GLOBAL 2000

"It reads like something out of "The Empire Strikes Back." The time: the year 2000. The place: Earth, a desolate planet slowly dying of its own accumulating follies. Half of the forests are gone; sand dunes spread where fertile farm lands once lay. Nearly 2 million species of plants, birds, insects and animals have vanished. Yet man is prop-agating so fast that his cities have grown as large as his nations of a century before. "

—Newsweek

"By now such grim warnings have become all too familiar. But this particular forecast is different. For the first time, the U.S. Government has added its full voice to the chorus of environmental Cassandras deeply distressed about the future."

—Time

"Compiled by more than a dozen Federal agencies, *Global 2000* is not a prediction but a projection—and a conservative one at that. It presents so immediate a challenge to worldwide political stability and American economic security that even the most complacent new administration must recognize it as a priority issue for the President and Congress."

—John B. Oakes, *The New York Times*

"[*Global 2000*] is first a warning to the world's citizens and their leaders. It attempts to mark the boundaries of a new task for the human race, to preserve life on this planet."

—Kansas City Star

Books by Gerald O. Barney

Studies for the 21st Century, Editor (with Martha J. Garrett and Jennie M. Hommel), (forthcoming, 1992).

Managing a Nation: The Microcomputer Software Catalog, Second Edition, Editor (with W. Brian Kreutzer and Martha J. Garrett), Westview Press (1991).

Christian Theology and the Future of Creation, the proceedings of a conference, Editor (with Carey Burkett), Holden Village Press (1990).

Estudios del Siglo 21, Editor (with A. Alonso), Editorial LIMUSA, Mexico, DF (1988).

Managing a Nation's 21st Century Study: A Handbook, (with Dr. Martha J. Garrett), Institute for 21st Century Studies, Inc. (1988).

The Future of the Creation: The Central Challenge for the Church, the proceedings of a symposium, Editor, Institute for 21st Century Studies, Inc. (1986).

Managing a Nation: The Software Sourcebook, Editor (with Sheryl Wilkins), Institute for 21st Century Studies, Inc. (1986).

Global 2000: Implications for Canada (with P. Freeman and C. Ulinsky), Pergamon Press (1981).

The Global 2000 Report to the President: Entering the Twenty-First Century, Editor and Study Director. Three volumes, U.S. Government Printing Office (1980). Also available in Spanish, Japanese, Chinese, German, Hungarian, Italian and French.

The Unfinished Agenda: The Citizen's Policy Guide to Environmental Issues, Editor and Task Force Chairman. Report of the task force sponsored by the Rockefeller Brothers Fund, Crowell Publishers (1977).

Foreword by Jimmy Carter

The Report

Global

to the President

2000

**ENTERING
THE
TWENTY-FIRST
CENTURY**

Gerald O. Barney

SEVEN LOCKS PRESS

About the Cover

The Global 2000 Report to the President presents a picture that can be painted only in broad strokes and with a brush still in need of additional bristles. It is, however, the most complete and consistent such picture ever painted by the U.S. Government. Many rapid and undesirable developments are foreseen if public policies concerning population stabilization, resource conservation, and environmental protection remain unchanged over the coming decades. Vigorous and determined new initiatives are needed around the world. These initiatives need to be taken soon while the picture is yet fluid and nations are still preparing to enter the twenty-first century.

Library of Congress Cataloging-in-Publication Data

Global 2000 : the report to the President—entering the twenty-first century / [edited by] Gerald O. Barney. — [Rev. ed.]
      p.   cm.
   Originally published as: The global 2000 report to the President—entering the twenty-first century, vol. 1, 1980; reissued in 1988.
Includes bibliographical references (p.   ) and index.
ISBN 0-932020-96-8 : $7.95
   1. Environmental policy. 2. Natural resources. 3. Food supply. 4. Twenty-first century—Forecasts. 5. Twentieth century—Forecasts 6. Economic forecasting.
I. Barney, Gerald O.   II. Global 2000 Study (U.S.). Global 2000 report to the President—entering the twenty-first century.   III. Title: Global two thousand.
HC79.E5G59 1991
333.7—dc20

91-35683
CIP

Printed by Thomson-Shore, Inc., Dexter, MI
Manufactured in the United States of America

For information write or call:

      Seven Locks Press
      P.O. Box 229
      Arlington, VA 22210
      (703) 243-2252

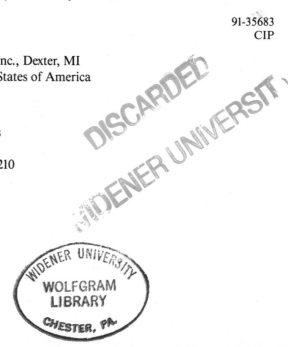

"I am directing the Council on Environmental Quality and the Department of State, working in cooperation with . . .other appropriate agencies, to make a one-year study of the probable changes in the world's population, natural resources, and environment through the end of the century."

President Jimmy Carter
May 23, 1977

CONTENTS

List of Tables

List of Figures

All figures, unless otherwise noted, are from *The Global Report to the President: Entering the Twenty-First Century*, vol. 2, *Technical Report*, Washington: Government Printing Office, 1980.

Foreword

by Jimmy Carter

With various political and economic interests competing throughout the world for influence, it's hard to find ways in which agriculture, health care, and environmental preservation can be pursued together.

It's easy to blame people who are cutting down trees. In countries such as Sudan, where in 1989 260,000 people died from war, or Ethiopia, or Somalia, or Mozambique—it's easy to say that if they can't prevent the civil war, somehow or another, they deserve to suffer. It's easy to blame them; it's easy to blame our own government, or outside sources, for the problems. We always know the answers for other people. But, ultimately, we not only want a good life for ourselves, we want a good life for others as well.

What is the mechanism, or the means, by which we can cross the chasm between ourselves and others around the world who can actually implement what we want to accomplish? I believe the means consist of establishing trust by producing results at the grassroots level, and by this immediate benefit convincing the political leadership of the world (including the leadership in this country) that long-term planning of food production, health care, and environmental preservation must be done together, as was envisioned in the process begun when I commissioned the Global 2000 report during my presidency. This one-year study assessed the probable changes in the world's population and environment through the end of the century and was to serve as the foundation of future planning.

At The Carter Center in Atlanta, we try to combine agriculture, health care, and environmental quality work in a number of places around the world. We have projects in China, Bangladesh, Pakistan, Tanzania, Uganda, Kenya, Ghana, Nigeria, Zambia, and other countries.

In the last twenty years, the per-capita production of food grain across Africa has actually gone down. The average African is now consuming seventy calories fewer per day than twenty years ago. Sometimes the leaders there have to be convinced, contrary to their natural inclination, that what we from The Carter Center are trying to do in health, population, environmental work, and food production is best for their country. I sit at the table with the king or the president or the prime minister, and because I was president they generally bring in all their cabinet officers. I bring with me people such as Dr. Norman Borlaug, who was a Nobel Laureate for his work in the green revolution, and the Carter Center's executive director, Dr. William Foege, who orchestrated the campaign to eradicate smallpox from the Earth, and we tell these leaders what we hope to accomplish in their country. Our purpose at that meeting is to get the country's key people convinced that what we're proposing can benefit them. If they're not convinced, then we are going to be dealing with third-level bureaucrats, not with key cabinet ministers. And nothing will be accomplished.

In January 1986 I made my first trip to Ghana, primarily to talk about food production. That year we got forty farmers to participate in our Global 2000 program. Twenty planted corn, and twenty planted sorghum; each planted about one acre of demonstration plots using traditional farming practices, and one acre using an improved kind of seed and a moderate amount of fertilizer. We didn't bring any mechanization; the farmers still plant with a pointed stick and cultivate with a hoe. But the demonstration plots were so successful—on average tripling the previous yield—that we jumped in 1987 from forty farmers to twelve hundred. In 1988, Global 2000 had sixteen thousand, and in 1989 eighty-five thousand Ghanaian farmers participating in our program.

We also teach farmers environmentally sound growing techniques. They plant now in contour rows, to stave off erosion. Instead of slash-and-burn techniques—where they would burn off an area of forest, plant it for one year, and then move on to another area—farmers now plant using enough fertilizer so that they can repeatedly grow crops on the same plot of land. That means the forest can be saved. And we have only three foreign employees in Ghana: two Mexicans and one Korean. All the rest of the workers are Ghanaians, so at the end of five years (1991) we plan to withdraw from Ghana, leaving that nation self-sufficient in food production.

Ethiopia is another example of a country in which we have to prove the immediate benefit of our work before we can get started on the road to long-term solutions. The war in Ethiopia between the government and the Eritrean People's Liberation Front—over whether Eritrea should be part of Ethiopia or have the right to self-determination—is twenty-nine years old. Both sides are Marxist. A million people have died in this war, not only as a result of bombs, bullets, and shells, but also from starvation, malnutrition, and diarrhea among children as a direct result of lack of food.

Ethiopia is the poorest country in the world, with a per-capita income of one hundred thirty dollars. Farmers there produce only four bags of grain per acre. It's impossible to get people in such poverty to worry about environmental issues. It's impossible to gain their confidence or forge partnerships with just words. They're starving. So what we at The Carter Center try to do first is get Dr. Borlaug's staff to show farmers how to triple or even quadruple production of grain per acre. When we show a direct and identifiable benefit to the people, the leaders see a political benefit, and that short-term gain gives them enough confidence in us to listen to environmental discussions. I might add that in spite of its being the poorest nation on Earth, Ethiopia spends 60 percent of its total national wealth on weapons.

It's easy to criticize the Third World for its burgeoning population, but deeply related to the problem of too many people is wasteful consumption. I have four children and six grandchildren. It's sobering to me to know that each one of them, and Rosalynn and I, consumes fifteen times as much of the world's limited resources as does the average citizen in India. When we worry about population growth in India, when we tell them they ought to be ashamed, we ought to remember that fifteen children in India are not going to deplete the world's supply of vital resources any more in the future than one child born in America. Perhaps, in addition to efforts directed at population control in India, we should exert some self-discipline to conserve resources. When I left office we had, after a lot of heartache and struggle, reduced our dependence on imported oil to about 30 percent of total use. Now it's back up to 50 percent, and going up every day. The developed world has got to realize that a large part of the responsibility to conserve resources is still ours.

We also need to change our dependence on weapons production and weapons sales overseas as a basic foundation for jobs in this country. It costs about one million dollars in defense expenditures to create one job—a vast inefficiency. But we have been so seduced, so influenced, so outspent—so outbribed, you might say—in the Congress of the United States by the defense industry that it's almost impossible to prevail when you want to cut back on unnecessary expenditures.

Another inefficiency: The US Agency for International Development program (USAID), which was supposed to be designed for sustainable development in the Third World, is almost totally incompetent. The Carnegie Foundation and The Carter Center, looking to the application of science and technology to improve the quality of life in the Third World, recently did a definitive analysis of USAID. Of the $11 billion spent annually, $10 million goes to Israel every day, about two thirds of that amount goes to Egypt, and a huge part of the remainder goes to finance purchases of weapons from American manufacturers. This leaves about $2.1 billion a year to actually improve the lives of people overseas. Of that $2.1 billion, 80 percent goes to administrative costs: It costs us eighty cents of every dollar to finance the expenditure of twenty cents of aid in the Third World.

Japan also budgets about $11 billion for overseas aid. What they do is go to the leaders of the poor nations and say, "We have $26 million to spend on health care in you country. What is the best way to spend it?" And with minimal administrative costs, with practically no staff in the country, they work harmoniously with that country's minister of health, spending the money for safe water or to provide immunization programs. This is not purely altruistic on the part of the Japanese, because they are planting small seeds of help that in the future will pay richly in friendship, partnership, and availability of increasingly scarce natural resources. They will also reap a benefit in commerce, creating markets for Japanese consumer products. You can't do that when you spend eighty cents of every dollar on administrative costs.

In working with the developing world, you see the relationships between health care and other problems, such as illiteracy. Here's an example, and an opportunity for people who work in telecommunications research and development:

A lot of the most arable land in the Third World has not even been planted because of two afflictions: Guinea worm and river blindness. Guinea worm, which most Americans have never heard of, affects ten million people a year. It's a parasite people get from drinking impure water. The water contains the worm's egg, and inside the human body that egg grows into a worm a meter long in twelve months. The worm then emerges through the skin, leaving a horrible sore.

River blindness is caused by the sting of a fly found along fast-flowing streams. Sometimes you go to villages where 35 percent of the adults are blind; you see adults walking around holding one end of a stick with a little five-year-old child holding the other end, acting as a seeing-eye baby. And you know that if something isn't done, that child will be blind someday, too.

We have treatments for both these conditions, donated by U.S. corporations such as Merck and Company, and we can go in with them. In fact, the Global 2000 program and other health care organizations have targeted 1995 as the year by which Guinea worm will be eradicated. But remember, we're trying to teach people to take care of themselves. So there's another problem: How do you educate people who are basically illiterate about the cause of Guinea worm or river blindness? We ran our first test case in Pakistan, in a place where only 12 percent of the men, and almost no women, were literate. There are currently two ways to communicate with these people. One is through radio, and the other is by giving them printed cartoon that tell the story in pictures. These are not very efficient methods, and so there's a need for telecommunications people to get involved, to invent a way to communicate health information to people who are illiterate. Long-term planners can see that these problems— health care and illiteracy—are related.

The world political situation, far from being hopeless, offers opportunities to help everywhere. I wish the major universities throughout the West would, in effect, adopt a Third World country. The University of Georgia has a great agricultural school and a great forestry school, and could go to a country such as Haiti and ask, "What can we do to help you to provide jobs, replant your forests, improve tourism, educate your people, build better homes, establish democracy?" Haiti would accept a university, whereas it would never accept any intrusion from the U.S. government (most countries won't, by the way). Working with major corporations in our country and others, the university could bring in students and give them an opportunity to help, and in the process those students would learn things about the developing world they might otherwise never know.

Rosalynn and I are volunteers with Habitat for Humanity, which builds housing for homeless people. In June we're going to Tijuana to build a hundred homes on a barren hillside in a desperately poor area. It's arid, so there aren't many trees. We've used wood, two-by-four studs, before. Now we're working on a problem: How are we going to build adobe block homes with inexperienced volunteers who lack masonry skills? We'll find a way, but the point is we'll do it with absolutely no government money, and in the process we'll develop innovative ways for inexperienced people, in arid parts of the world at least, to build homes at a very low cost.

I would like to see the Global 2000 process revived. It was killed when I left Washington because of a political aversion to long-term planning with an emphasis on the environment. It ought to be resurrected and concentrated in the National Academy of Sciences, not in the federal government. It ought to be supported by the major corporations. It wouldn't take much money. This we can do collectively, as men and women committed to sustainable development, to a better quality of life, for all those on Earth.

I don't have any sense of impending doom or despair. I think that things can be changed. If you look at the face of just one Ghanaian farmer who for the first time is producing sixteen bags of sorghum or corn where previously there were just three or four bags, and see how eager he is to join our program of environmental work as well, you know the Third World is not a hopeless place. The people there are waiting to be partners with people here in seeing that everybody on Earth can have a better way of life.

Preface to the Revised Edition

Since its publication in 1980, *The Global 2000 Report to the President* has become a minor classic. More than 1.5 million copies have been sold. Volume I has been published in English, French, German, Japanese, Chinese, Hungarian, Spanish, and Italian; Volume II (776 pages) has been published in English, Spanish, German, Japanese, and Chinese. The highly technical Volume III has been published only in English.

The enduring value of *Global 2000* is due not only to its demographic, economic, resource, and environmental projections, but also to the integration of those projections. Prior to its publication, no national government had ever issued such a comprehensive, integrated analysis of the global future.

No national government has yet produced a report comparable to *Global 2000*, but many nations have undertaken integrated studies of their own national future. Many are modeled, in part, on the *Global 2000* work. These new national analyses are generally referred to as twenty-first-century studies.

Such studies are critical for countries struggling to survive complex challenges that include economic development, population growth, resource depletion, and environmental deterioration. These interrelated issues not only can lead to social disruptions, economic instability, and political unrest within individual countries, but also can be a major cause of tension and armed conflict across national borders.

Throughout the world there are many governmental units, including planning agencies, that address economic, demographic, resource, and environmental issues through plans and analyses that look ahead up to five years. Unfortunately, short-term approaches usually fail to take into account adequately the linkages among sectors and, as a consequence, eventually lead to other, often more serious, problems.

Fortunately, there is growing recognition by leaders around the world that global and national prosperity will require long-term strategies rather than quick-fix solutions. These leaders have appointed task forces to analyze alternative national futures in terms of their sustainability. The teams are usually headed by someone of considerable political stature, often a top governmental minister, and they all include professionals from a variety of backgrounds. Such groups, often called "21st century study teams," have been established or are forming in over 30 nations.

The twenty-first-century studies do not predict the future; rather, they provide detailed factual information and projections that help people make choices today that lead to the future they desire. These studies differ in three important ways from the routine research done by planning agencies. First, they examine many major global sectors in an integrated way: they project future trends in such areas as trade, foreign debt, demography, natural resources, environment, technology, health, education, and security, and they look at ways in which these areas interact. Second, these studies take a long-term approach rather than limiting their perspectives to "five-year" plans. This is critical since the importance of some trends and their intersectoral linkages is much more apparent in projections that extend for a decade or two. Third, these studies evaluate alternative futures in terms of economic, ecological, political, and social sustainability. They continually address the question, "Will this development strategy lead to a healthy situation in the long run, or will it have troublesome consequences after a few years?"

The Institute for 21st Century Studies was founded to encourage and support such studies through training and other assistance [see Appendix C]. Among our training materials is a handbook on how to conduct a twenty-first-century study and a sourcebook on microcomputer software for managing a nation's future. Volume I of *The Global 2000 Report* has also been a useful instructional tool.

Unfortunately, *The Global 2000 Report to the President* is no longer available from the U.S. Government Printing Office. The last copies of Volume I were sold in early 1988. Volume III sold out in 1987, and less than 100 copies of Volume II remain unsold at this writing. Pergamon Press still has copies of an edition consisting of Volume I plus the most important parts of Volume II, and Penguin has copies of an edition combining Volume I and the full Volume II.

Because of Volume I's importance and because it continues to be used in many university courses, the Institute and Seven Locks Press has decided to bring out this revised version of Volume I.

Martha J. Garrett
Co-Director
Institute for 21st Century Studies

Gerald O. Barney
Co-Director
Institute for 21st Century Studies
Study Director for the *Global 2000* study

Preface to First Edition

Environmental problems do not stop at national boundaries. In the past decade, we and other nations have come to recognize the urgency of international efforts to protect our common environment.

As part of this process, I am directing the Council on Environmental Quality and the Department of State, working in cooperation with the Environmental Protection Agency, the National Science Foundation, the National Oceanic and Atmospheric Administration, and other appropriate agencies, to make a one-year study of the probable changes in the world's population, natural resources, and environment through the end of the century. This study will serve as the foundation of our longer-term planning.

President Carter issued this directive in his Environmental Message to the Congress on May 23, 1977. It marked the beginning of what became a three-year effort to discover the long-term implications of present world trends in population, natural resources, and the environment and to assess the Government's foundation for long-range planning.

Government concern with trends in population, resources, and environment is not new. Indeed, study of these issues by Federal commissions and planning boards extends back at least 70 years.[1] The earlier studies, however, tended to view each issue without relation to the others, to limit their inquiries to the borders of this nation and the short-term future, and to have relatively little effect on policy.[2] What is new in more recent studies is a growing awareness of the interdependence of population, resources, and environment. The Global 2000 Study is the first U.S. Government effort to look at all three issues from a long-term global perspective that recognizes their interrelationships and attempts to make connections among them.

The Global 2000 Study is reported in three volumes. This Summary is the first volume. Volume II, the Technical Report, presents the Study in further detail and is referenced extensively in this Summary. The third volume provides technical documentation on the Government's global models.

Major Findings and Conclusions intro

If present trends continue, the world in 2000 will be more crowded, more polluted, less stable ecologically, and more vulnerable to disruption than the world we live in now. Serious stresses involving population, resources, and environment are clearly visible ahead. Despite greater material output, the world's people will be poorer in many ways than they are today.

For hundreds of millions of the desperately poor, the outlook for food and other necessities of life will be no better. For many it will be worse. Barring revolutionary advances in technology, life for most people on earth will be more precarious in 2000 than it is now—unless the nations of the world act decisively to alter current trends.

This, in essence, is the picture emerging from the U.S. Government's projections of probable changes in world population, resources, and environment by the end of the century, as presented in the Global 2000 Study. They do not predict what will occur. Rather, they depict conditions that are likely to develop if there are no changes in public policies, institutions, or rates of technological advance, and if there are no wars or other major disruptions. A keener awareness of the nature of the current trends, however, may induce changes that will alter these trends and the projected outcome.

Principal Findings

Rapid growth in world population will hardly have altered by 2000. The world's population will grow from 4 billion in 1975 to 6.35 billion in 2000, an increase of more than 50 percent. The rate of growth will slow only marginally, from 1.8 percent a year to 1.7 percent. In terms of sheer numbers, population will be growing faster in 2000 than it is today, with 100 million people added each year compared with 75 million in 1975. Ninety percent of this growth will occur in the poorest countries.

While the economies of the less developed countries (LDCs) are expected to grow at faster rates than those of the industrialized nations, the gross national product per capita in most LDCs remains low. The average gross national product per capita is projected to rise substantially in some LDCs (especially in Latin America), but in the great populous nations of South Asia it remains below $200 a year (in 1975 dollars). The large existing gap between the rich and poor nations widens.

World food production is projected to increase 90 percent over the 30 years from 1970 to 2000. This translates into a global per capita increase of less than 15 percent over the same period. The bulk of that increase goes to countries that already have relatively high per capita food consumption. Meanwhile per capita consumption in South Asia, the Middle East, and the LDCs of Africa will scarcely improve or will actually decline below present inadequate levels. At the same time, real prices for food are expected to double.

Arable land will increase only 4 percent by 2000, so that most of the increased output of food will have to come from higher yields. Most of the elements that now contribute to higher yields—fertilizer, pesticides, power for irrigation, and fuel for machinery—depend heavily on oil and gas.

During the 1990s world oil production will approach geological estimates of maximum production capacity, even with rapidly increasing petroleum prices. The Study projects that the richer industrialized nations will be able to command enough oil and other commercial energy supplies to meet rising demands through 1990. With the expected price increases, many less developed countries will have increasing difficulties meeting energy needs. For the one-quarter of humankind that depends primarily on wood for fuel, the outlook is bleak. Needs for fuelwood will exceed available supplies by about 25 percent before the turn of the century.

While the world's finite fuel resources—coal, oil, gas, oil shale, tar sands, and uranium—are theoretically sufficient for centuries, they are not evenly distributed; they pose difficult economic and environmental problems; and they vary greatly in their amenability to exploitation and use.

Nonfuel mineral resources generally appear sufficient to meet projected demands through 2000, but further discoveries and investments will be needed to maintain reserves. In addition, production costs will increase with energy prices and may make some nonfuel mineral resources uneconomic. The quarter of the world's population that inhabits industrial countries will continue to absorb three-fourths of the world's mineral production.

Regional water shortages will become more severe. In the 1970–2000 period population growth alone will cause requirements for water to double in nearly half the world. Still greater increases would be needed to improve standards of living. In many LDCs, water supplies will become increasingly erratic by 2000 as a result of extensive deforestation. Development of new water supplies will become more costly virtually everywhere.

Significant losses of world forests will continue over the next 20 years as demand for forest products and fuelwood increases. Growing stocks of commercial-size timber are projected to decline 50 percent per capita. The world's forests are now disappearing at the rate of 18–20 million hectares a year (an area half the size of California), with most of the loss occurring in the humid tropical forests of Africa, Asia, and South America. The projections indicate that by 2000 some 40 percent of the remaining forest cover in LDCs will be gone.

Serious deterioration of agricultural soils will occur worldwide, due to erosion, loss of organic matter, desertification, salinization, alkalinization, and waterlogging. Already, an area of cropland and grassland approximately the size of Maine is becoming barren wasteland each year, and the spread of desert-like conditions is likely to accelerate.

Atmospheric concentrations of carbon dioxide and ozone-depleting chemicals are expected to increase at rates that could alter the world's climate and upper atmosphere significantly by 2050. Acid rain from increased combustion of fossil fuels (especially coal) threatens damage to lakes, soils, and crops. Radioactive and other hazardous materials present health and safety problems in increasing numbers of countries.

Extinctions of plant and animal species will increase dramatically. Hundreds of thousands of species—perhaps as many as 20 percent of all species on earth—will be irretrievably lost as their habitats vanish, especially in tropical forests.

The future depicted by the U.S. Government projections, briefly outlined above, may actually understate the impending problems. The methods available for carrying out the Study led to certain gaps and inconsistencies that tend to impart an optimistic bias. For example, most of the individual projections for the various sectors studied—food, minerals, energy, and so on—assume that sufficient capital, energy, water, and land will be available in each of these sectors to meet their needs, regardless of the competing needs of the other sectors. More consistent, better-integrated projections would produce a still more emphatic picture of intensifying stresses, as the world enters the twenty-first century.

Conclusions

At present and projected growth rates, the world's population would reach 10 billion by 2030 and would approach 30 billion by the end of the twenty-first century. These levels correspond closely to estimates by the U.S. National Academy of Sciences of the maximum carrying capacity of the entire earth. Already the populations in sub-Saharan Africa and in the Himalayan hills of Asia have exceeded the carrying capacity of the immediate area, triggering an erosion of the land's capacity to support life. The resulting poverty and ill health have further complicated efforts to reduce fertility. Unless this circle of interlinked problems is broken soon, population growth in such areas will unfortunately be slowed for reasons other than declining birth rates. Hunger and disease will claim more babies and young children, and more of those surviving will be mentally and physically handicapped by childhood malnutrition.

Indeed, the problems of preserving the carrying capacity of the earth and sustaining the possibility of a decent life for the human beings that inhabit it are enormous and close upon us. Yet there is reason for hope. It must be emphasized that the Global 2000 Study's projections are based on the assumption that national policies regarding population stabilization, resource conservation, and environmental protection will remain essentially unchanged through the end of the century. But in fact, policies are beginning to change. In some areas, forests are being replanted after cutting. Some nations are taking steps to reduce soil losses and desertification. Interest in energy conservation is growing, and large sums are being invested in exploring alternatives to petroleum dependence. The need for family planning is slowly becoming better understood. Water supplies are being improved and waste treatment systems built. High-yield seeds are widely available and seed banks are being expanded. Some wildlands with their genetic resources are being protected. Natural predators and selective pesticides are being substituted for persistent and destructive pesticides.

Encouraging as these developments are, they are far from adequate to meet the global challenges projected in this Study. Vigorous, determined new initiatives are needed if worsening poverty and human suffering, environmental degradation, and international tension and conflicts are to be prevented. There are no quick fixes. The only solutions to the problems of population, resources, and environment are complex and long-term. These problems are inextricably linked to some of the most perplexing and persistent problems in the world—poverty, injustice, and social conflict. New and imaginative ideas—and a willingness to act on them—are essential.

The needed changes go far beyond the capability and responsibility of this or any other single nation. An era of unprecedented cooperation and commitment is essential. Yet there are opportunities—and a strong rationale —for the United States to provide leadership among nations. A high priority for this Nation must be a thorough assessment of its foreign and domestic policies relating to population, resources, and environment. The United States, possessing the world's largest economy, can expect its policies to have a significant influence on global trends. An equally important priority for the United States is to cooperate generously and justly with other nations—particularly in the areas of trade, investment, and assistance—in seeking solutions to the many problems that extend beyond our national boundaries. There are many unfulfilled opportunities to cooperate with other nations in efforts to relieve poverty and hunger, stabilize population, and enhance economic and environmental productivity. Further cooperation among nations is also needed to strengthen international mechanisms for protecting and utilizing the "global commons"—the oceans and atmosphere.

To meet the challenges described in this Study, the United States must improve its ability to identify emerging problems and assess alternative responses. In using and evaluting the Government's present capability for long-term global analysis, the Study found serious inconsistencies in the methods and assumptions employed by the various agencies in making their projections. The Study itself made a start toward resolving these inadequacies. It represents the Government's first attempt to produce an interrelated set of population, resource, and environmental projections, and it has brought forth the most consistent set of global projections yet achieved by U.S. agencies. Nevertheless, the projections still contain serious gaps and contradictions that must be corrected if the Government's analytic capability is to be improved. It must be acknowledged that at present the Federal agencies are not always capable of providing projections of the quality needed for long-term policy decisions.

While limited resources may be a contributing factor in some instances, the primary problem is lack of coordination. The U.S. Government needs a mechanism for continuous review of the assumptions and methods the Federal agencies use in their projection models and for assurance that the agencies' models are sound, consistent, and well documented. The improved analyses that could result would provide not only a clearer sense of emerging problems and opportunities, but also a better means for evaluating alternative responses, and a better basis for decisions of worldwide significance that the President, the Congress, and the Federal Government as a whole must make.

With its limitations and rough approximations, the Global 2000 Study may be seen as no more than a reconnaissance of the future; nonetheless its conclusions are reinforced by similar findings of other recent global studies that were examined in the course of the Global 2000 Study (see Appendix). All these studies are in general agreement on the nature of the problems and on the threats they pose to the future welfare of humankind. The available evidence leaves no doubt that the world—including this Nation—faces enormous, urgent, and complex problems in the decades immediately ahead. Prompt and vigorous changes in public policy around the world are needed to avoid or minimize these problems before they become unmanageable. Long lead times are required for effective action. If decisions are delayed until the problems become worse, options for effective action will be severely reduced.

The Study in Brief

The President's directive establishing the Global 2000 Study called for a "study of the probable changes in the world's population, natural resources, and environment through the end of the century" and indicated that the Study as a whole was to "serve as the foundation of our longer-term planning."[3] The findings of the Study identify problems to which world attention must be directed. But because all study reports eventually become dated and less useful, the Study's findings alone cannot provide the foundation called for in the directive. The necessary foundation for longer-term planning lies not in study findings *per se*, but in the Government's continuing institutional capabilities—skilled personnel, data, and analytical models—for developing studies and analyses. Therefore, to meet the objectives stated in the President's directive, the Global 2000 Study was designed not only to assess probable changes in the world's population, natural resources, and environment, but also, through the study process itself, to identify and strengthen the Government's capability for longer-term planning and analysis.[4]

Building the Study

The process chosen for the Global 2000 Study was to develop trend projections using, to the fullest extent possible, the long-term global data and models routinely employed by the Federal agencies. The process also included a detailed analysis of the Government's global modeling capabilities as well as a comparison of the Government's findings with those of other global analyses.

An executive group, established and co-chaired by the Council on Environmental Quality and the State Department, together with a team of designated agency coordinators, assisted in locating the agencies' experts, data, and analytical models. A number of Americans from outside Government and several people from other countries advised on the study structure. The agencies' expert met occasionally with some of these advisers to work out methods for coordinating data, models, and assumptions.

Overall, the Federal agencies have an impressive capability for long-term analyses of world trends in population, resources, and environment. Several agencies have extensive, richly detailed data bases and highly elaborate sectoral models. Collectively, the agencies' sectoral models and data constitute the Nation's present foundation for long-term planning and analysis.[5]

Currently, the principal limitation in the Government's long-term global analytical capability is that the models for various sectors were not designed to be used together in a consistent and interactive manner. The agencies' models were created at different times, using different methods, to meet different objectives. Little thought has been given to how the various sectoral models—and the institutions of which they are a part—can be related to each other to project a comprehensive, consistent image of the world. As a result, there has been little direct interaction among the agencies' sectoral models.[6]

With the Government's current models, the individual sectors addressed in the Global 2000 Study could be interrelated only by developing projections sequentially, that is, by using the results of some of the projections as inputs to others. Since population and gross national product (GNP) projections were required to estimate demand in the resource sector models, the population and GNP projections were developed first, in 1977. The resource projections followed in late 1977 and early 1978. All of the projections were linked to the environment projections, which were made during 1978 and 1979.[7]

The Global 2000 Study developed its projections in a way that furthered interactions, improved internal consistency, and generally strengthened the Government's global models. However, the effort to harmonize and integrate the Study's projections was only partially successful. Many internal contradictions and inconsistencies could not be resolved. Inconsistencies arose immediately from the fact that sequential projections are not as interactive as events in the real world, or as projections that could be achieved in an improved model. While the sequential process allowed some interaction among the model's sectors, it omitted the continuous influence that all the elements—population, resources, economic activity, environment—have upon each other. For example, the Global 2000 Study food projections assume that the catch from traditional fisheries will increase as fast as world population, while the fisheries projections indicate that this harvest will not increase over present levels on a sustainable basis. If it has been possible to link the fisheries and food projections, the expected fisheries contribution to the human food supply could have been realistically reflected in the food projections. This and other inconsistencies are discussed in detail in the Technical Report.[8]

Difficulties also arise from multiple allocation of resources. Most of the quantitative projections simply assume that resource needs in the sector they cover—needs for capital, energy, land, water, minerals—will be met. Since the needs for each sector are not clearly identified, they cannot be summed up and compared with estimates of what might be available. It is very likely that the same resources have been allocated to more than one sector.[9]

Equally significant, some of the Study's resource projections implicitly assume that the goods and services provided in the past by the earth's land, air, and water will continue to be available in larger and larger amounts, with no maintenance problems and no increase in costs. The Global 2000 Study projections for the environment cast serious doubt on these assumptions.[10]

Collectively, the inconsistencies and missing linkages that are unavoidable with the Government's current global models affect the Global 2000 projections in many ways. Analysis of the assumptions underlying the projections and comparisons with other global projections suggest that most of the Study's quantitative results understate the severity of potential problems the world will face as it prepares to enter the twenty-first century.[11]

The question naturally arises as to whether circumstances have changed significantly since the earliest projections were made in 1977. The answer is no. What changes have occurred generally support the projections and highlight the problems identified. The brief summaries of the projections (beginning on the next page) each conclude with comments on how the projections might be altered if redeveloped today.

The Global 2000 Study has three major underlying assumptions. First, the projections assume a general continuation around the world of present public policy relating to population stabilization, natural resource conservation, and environmental protection.* The projections thus point to the expected future if policies continue without significant changes.

The second major assumption relates to the effects of technological developments and of the market mechanism. The Study assumes that rapid rates of technological development and adoption will continue, and that the rate of development will be spurred on by efforts to deal with problems identified by this Study. Participating agencies were asked to use the technological assumptions they normally use in preparing long-term global projections. In general, the agencies assume a continuation of rapid rates of technological development and no serious social resistance to the adoption of new technologies. Agricultural technology, for example, is assumed to continue increasing crop yields as rapidly as during the past few decades, including the period of the Green Revolution (see Figure 1). The projections assume no revolutionary advances—such as immediate wide-scale availability of nuclear fusion for energy production—and no disastrous setbacks—such as serious new health risks from widely used contraceptives or an outbreak of plant disease severely affecting an important strain of grain. The projections all assume that price, operating through the market mechanism, will reduce demand whenever supply constraints are encountered.[12]

Third, the Study assumes that there will be no major disruptions of international trade as a result

---

*There are a few important exceptions to this rule. For example, the population projections anticipate shifts in public policy that will provide significantly increased access to family planning services. (See Chapter 14 of the Technical Report for further details.)

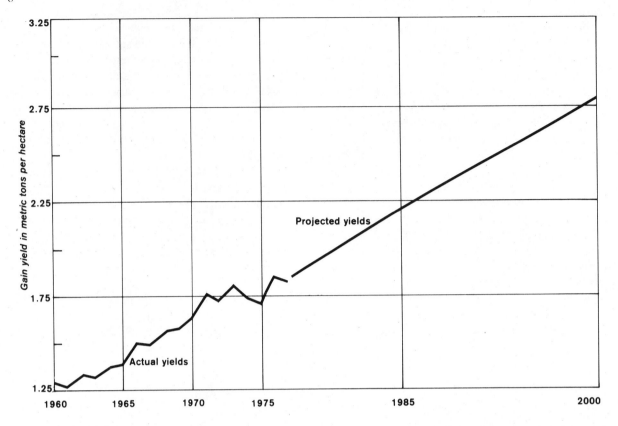

Figure 1. Historic and projected grain yields, 1960–2000. The food projections assume a continued rapid development and adoption of agricultural technology, much of it heavily dependent on fossil fuels.

of war, disturbance of the international monetary system, or political disruption. The findings of the Study do, however, point to increasing potential for international conflict and increasing stress on international financial arrangements. Should wars or a significant disturbance of the international monetary system occur, the projected trends would be altered in unpredictable ways.[13]

Because of the limitations outlined above, the Global 2000 Study is not the definitive study of future population, resource, and environment conditions. Nor is it intended to be a prediction. The Study does provide the most internally consistent and interrelated set of global projections available so far from the U.S. Government. Furthermore, its major findings are supported by a variety of nongovernmental global studies based on more highly interactive models that project similar trends through the year 2000 or beyond.[14]

Population and Income

Population and income projections provided the starting point for the Study. These projections were used wherever possible in the resource projections to estimate demand.

Population

One of the most important findings of the Global 2000 Study is that enormous growth in the world's population will occur by 2000 under any of the wide range of assumptions considered in the Study. The world's population increases 55 percent from 4.1 billion people in 1975 to 6.35 billion by 2000, under the Study's medium-growth projections.* While there is some uncertainty in these numbers, even the lowest-growth population projection shows a 46 percent increase—to 5.9 billion people by the end of the century.[15]

Another important finding is that the rapid growth of the world's population will not slow appreciably. The rate of growth per year in 1975 was 1.8 percent; the projected rate for 2000 is 1.7 per-

---

*Most of the projections in the Technical Report—including the population projections—provide a high, medium, and low series. Generally, only the medium series are discussed in this Summary Report.

cent. Even under the lowest growth projected, the number of persons being added annually to the world's population will be significantly greater in 2000 than today.[16]

Most of the population growth (92 percent) will occur in the less developed countries rather than in the industrialized countries. Of the 6.35 billion people in the world in 2000, 5 billion will live in LDCs. The LDCs' share of the world's population increased from 66 percent in 1950 to 72 percent in 1975, and is expected to reach 79 percent by 2000. LDC population growth rates will drop slightly, from 2.2 percent a year in 1975 to 2 percent in 2000, compared with 0.7 percent and 0.5 percent in developed countries. In some LDCs,

growth rates will still be more than 3 percent a year in 2000. Table 1 summarizes the population projections. Figure 2 shows the distribution of the world's population in 1975 and 2000.[17]

Figure 3 shows the age structure of the population in less developed and industrialized nations for 1975 and 2000. While the structures shown for the industrialized nations become more column-shaped (characteristic of a mature and slowly growing population), the structures for the LDCs remain pyramid-shaped (characteristic of rapid growth). The LDC populations, predominantly young with their childbearing years ahead of them, have a built-in momentum for further growth. Because of this momentum, a world

TABLE 1
Population Projections for World, Major Regions, and Selected Countries

	1975	2000	Percent Increase by 2000	Average Annual Percent Increase	Percent of World Population in 2000
	millions				
World	4,090	6,351	55	1.8	100
More developed regions	1,131	1,323	17	0.6	21
Less developed regions	2,959	5,028	70	2.1	79
Major regions					
Africa	399	814	104	2.9	13
Asia and Oceania	2,274	3,630	60	1.9	57
Latin America	325	637	96	2.7	10
U.S.S.R. and Eastern Europe	384	460	20	0.7	7
North America, Western Europe, Japan, Australia, and New Zealand	708	809	14	0.5	13
Selected countries and regions					
People's Republic of China	935	1,329	42	1.4	21
India	618	1,021	65	2.0	16
Indonesia	135	226	68	2.1	4
Bangladesh	79	159	100	2.8	2
Pakistan	71	149	111	3.0	2
Philippines	43	73	71	2.1	1
Thailand	42	75	77	2.3	1
South Korea	37	57	55	1.7	1
Egypt	37	65	77	2.3	1
Nigeria	63	135	114	3.0	2
Brazil	109	226	108	2.9	4
Mexico	60	131	119	3.1	2
United States	214	248	16	0.6	4
U.S.S.R.	254	309	21	0.8	5
Japan	112	133	19	0.7	2
Eastern Europe	130	152	17	0.6	2
Western Europe	344	378	10	0.4	6

Source: Global 2000 Technical Report, Table 2-10.

10

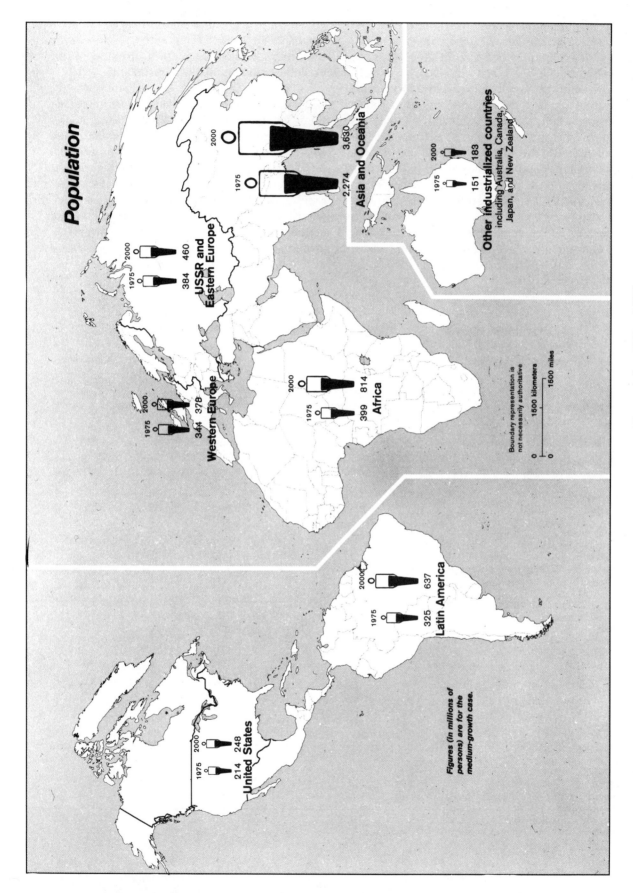

Figure 2. Distribution of the world's population, 1975 and 2000.

11

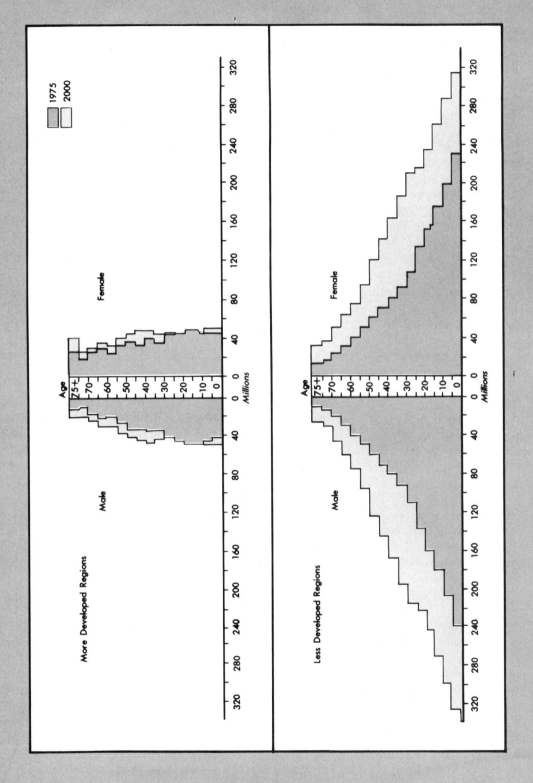

Figure 3. Age-sex composition of the world's population, medium series, 1975 and 2000.

12

population of around 6 billion is a virtual certainty for 2000 even if fertility rates were somehow to drop quickly to replacement levels (assuming there are no disastrous wars, famine, or pestilence).[18]

The projected fertility rates and life expectancies, together with the age structure of the world's population, are extremely significant for later years since these factors influence how soon world population could cease to grow and what the ultimate stabilized global population could be. The Study's projections assume that world fertility rates will drop more than 20 percent over the 1975-2000 period, from an average of 4.3 children per fertile woman to 3.3. In LDCs, fertility rates are projected to drop 30 percent as a result of moderate progress in social and economic development and increased availability and use of contraceptive methods. The projections also assume that life expectancies at birth for the world will increase 11 percent, to 65.5 years, as a result of improved health. The projected increases in life expectancies and decreases in fertility rates produce roughly counterbalancing demographic effects.[19]

In addition to rapid population growth, the LDCs will experience dramatic movements of rural populations to cities and adjacent settlements. If present trends continue, many LDC cities will become almost inconceivably large and crowded. By 2000, Mexico City is projected to have more than 30 million people— roughly three times the present population of the New York metropolitan area. Calcutta will approach 20 million. Greater Bombay, Greater Cairo, Jakarta, and Seoul are all expected to be in the 15-20 million range, and 400 cities will have passed the million mark.[20] Table 2 shows present and projected populations for 12 LDC cities.

Rapid urban growth will put extreme pressures on sanitation, water supplies, health care, food, shelter, and jobs. LDCs will have to increase urban services approximately two-thirds by 2000 just to stay even with 1975 levels of service per capita. The majority of people in large LDC cities are likely to live in "uncontrolled settlements"— slums and shantytowns where sanitation and other public services are minimal at best. In many large cities—for example, Bombay, Calcutta, Mexico City, Rio de Janeiro, Seoul, Taipei—a quarter or more of the population already lives in uncontrolled settlements, and the trend is sharply upward. It is not certain whether the trends projected

TABLE 2

Estimates and Rough Projections of Selected Urban Agglomerations in Developing Countries

	1960	1970	1975	2000
	Millions of persons			
Calcutta	5.5	6.9	8.1	19.7
Mexico City	4.9	8.6	10.9	31.6
Greater Bombay	4.1	5.8	7.1	19.1
Greater Cairo	3.7	5.7	6.9	16.4
Jakarta	2.7	4.3	5.6	16.9
Seoul	2.4	5.4	7.3	18.7
Delhi	2.3	3.5	4.5	13.2
Manila	2.2	3.5	4.4	12.7
Tehran	1.9	3.4	4.4	13.8
Karachi	1.8	3.3	4.5	15.9
Bogota	1.7	2.6	3.4	9.5
Lagos	0.8	1.4	2.1	9.4

Source: Global 2000 Technical Report, Table 13-9.

for enormous increases in LDC urban populations will in fact continue for 20 years. In the years ahead, lack of food for the urban poor, lack of jobs, and increasing illness and misery may slow the growth of LDC cities and alter the trend.[21]

Difficult as urban conditions are, conditions in rural areas of many LDCs are generally worse. Food, water, health, and income problems are often most severe in outlying agricultural and grazing areas. In some areas rural-urban migration and rapid urban growth are being accelerated by deteriorating rural conditions.[22]

An updated medium-series population projection would show little change from the Global 2000 Study projections. World population in 2000 would be estimated at about 6.18 (as opposed to 6.35) billion, a reduction of less than 3 percent. The expectation would remain that, in absolute numbers, population will be growing more rapidly by the end of the century than today.[23]

The slight reduction in the population estimate is due primarily to new data suggesting that fertility rates in some areas have declined a little more rapidly than earlier estimates indicated. The new data indicate that fertility declines have occurred in some places even in the absence of overall socioeconomic progress.[24] Between 1970 and 1976, for example, in the presence of extreme poverty and malnutrition, fertility declines of 10-15 percent occurred in Indonesia and 15-20 percent in the poorest income classes in Brazil.[25]

Income

Projected declines in fertility rates are based in part on anticipated social and economic progress, which is ultimately reflected in increased income. Income projections were not possible, and gross national product projections were used as surrogates. GNP, a rough and inadequate measure of social and economic welfare, is projected to increase worldwide by 145 percent over 25 years from 1975 to 2000. But because of population growth, per capita GNP increases much more slowly, from $1,500 in 1975 to $2,300 in 2000—an increase of 53 percent. For both the poorer and the richer countries, rates of growth in GNP are projected to decelerate after 1985.[26]

GNP growth is expected to be faster in LDCs (an average annual growth of 4.5 percent, or an approximate tripling over 25 years) than in developed regions (an average annual growth of 3.3 percent, or somewhat more than a doubling). However, the LDC growth in gross national product develops from a very low base, and population growth in the LDCs brings per capita increases in GNP down to very modest proportions. While parts of the LDC world, especially several countries in Latin America, are projected to improve significantly in per capita GNP by 2000, other countries will make little or no gains from their present low levels. India, Bangladesh, and Pakistan, for example, increase their per capita GNP by 31 percent, 8 percent, and 3 percent, respectively, but in all three countries GNP per capita remains below $200 (in 1975 dollars).[27] Figure 4 shows projected per capita gross national product by regions in 2000.

The present income disparities between the wealthiest and poorest nations are projected to widen. Assuming that present trends continue, the group of industrialized countries will have a per capita GNP of nearly $8,500 (in 1975 dollars) in 2000, and North America, Western Europe, Australia, New Zealand, and Japan will average more than $11,000. By contrast, per capita GNP in the LDCs will average less than $600. For every $1 increase in GNP per capita in the LDCs, a $20 increase is projected for the industrialized countries.[28] Table 3 and 4 summarize the GNP projections. The disparity between the developed countries and the less developed group is so marked that dramatically different rates of change would be needed to reduce the gap significantly by the end of the century.* Disparities between the rich and poor of many LDCs are equally striking.

Updated GNP projections would indicate somewhat lower economic growth than shown in the Global 2000 projections. Projections for the member nations of the Organization for Economic Cooperation and Development (OECD) have been revised downward over the past 2–3 years because of the effects of increasing petroleum prices and because of anticipated measures to reduce inflation. In turn, depressed growth in the OECD economies is expected to lead to slowed growth in LDC economies. For example, in 1976 the World Bank projected that the industrialized nations' economies would expand at 4.9 percent annually over the 1980–85 period; by 1979 the Bank had revised these projections downward to 4.2 percent annually over the 1980–90 period. Similarly, between 1976 and 1979 Bank projections for LDC economies dropped from 6.3 percent (1980-85 period) to 5.6 percent (1980-90 period).[29]

Resources

The Global 2000 Study resource projections are based to the fullest extent possible on the population and GNP projections presented previously. The resource projections cover food, fisheries, forests, nonfuel minerals, water, and energy.

Food

The Global 2000 Study projects world food production to increase at an average annual rate of about 2.2 percent over the 1970-2000 period. This rate of increase is roughly equal to the record growth rates experienced during the 1950s, 1960s, and early 1970s, including the period of the so-called Green Revolution. Assuming no deterioration in climate or weather, food production is projected to be 90 percent higher in 2000 than in 1970.[30]

*The gap would be significantly smaller—in some cases it would be reduced by about one half—if the comparison were based on purchasing power considerations rather than exchange rates, but a large gap would remain. (See I. B. Kravis et al., *International Comparisons of Real Product and Purchasing Power*, Baltimore: Johns Hopkins University Press. 1978.)

14

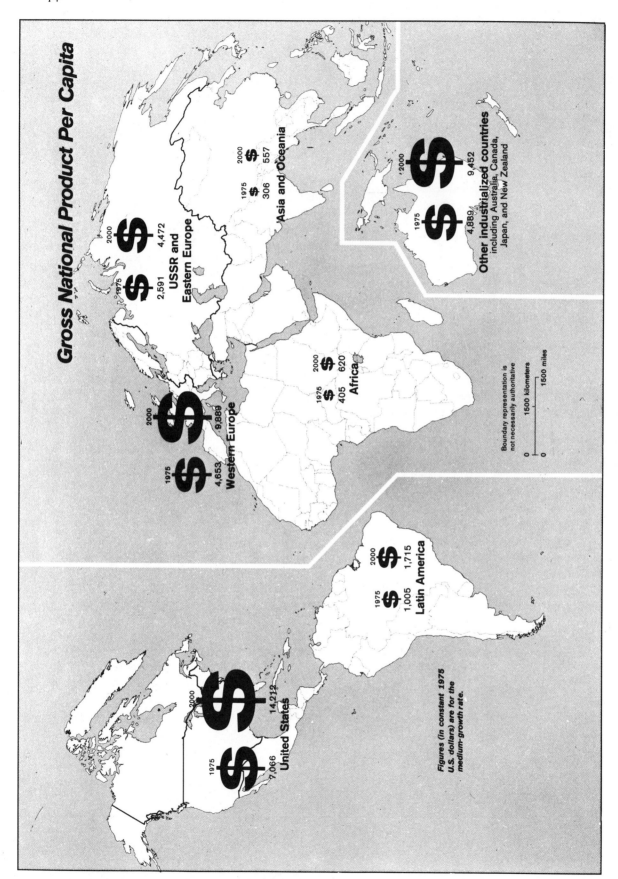

Figure 4. Per capita gross national product, by regions, 1975 and 2000.

TABLE 3
GNP Estimates (1975) and Projections and Growth Rates (1985, 2000) by Major Regions and Selected Countries and Regions

(Billions of constant 1975 dollars)

	1975 GNP	1975–85 Growth Rate	1985 Projections[a]	1985–2000 Growth Rate	2000 Projections[a]
		percent		*percent*	
WORLD	6,025	4.1	8,991	3.3	14,677
More developed regions	4,892	3.9	7,150	3.1	11,224
Less developed regions	1,133	5.0	1,841	4.3	3,452
MAJOR REGIONS					
Africa	162	5.2	268	4.3	505
Asia and Oceania	697	4.6	1,097	4.2	2,023
Latin America[b]	326	5.6	564	4.5	1,092
U.S.S.R. and Eastern Europe	996	3.3	1,371	2.8	2,060
North America, Western Europe, Japan, Australia, and New Zealand	3,844	4.0	5,691	3.1	8,996
SELECTED COUNTRIES AND REGIONS[c]					
People's Republic of China	286	3.8	413	3.8	718
India	92	3.6	131	2.8	198
Indonesia	24	6.4	45	5.4	99
Bangladesh	9	3.6	13	2.8	19
Pakistan	10	3.6	14	2.8	21
Philippines	16	5.6	27	4.4	52
Thailand	15	5.6	25	4.4	48
South Korea	19	5.6	32	4.4	61
Egypt	12	5.6	20	4.4	38
Nigeria	23	6.4	43	5.4	94
Brazil	108	5.6	185	4.4	353
Mexico	71	5.6	122	4.4	233
United States[d]	1,509	4.0	2,233	3.1	3,530
U.S.S.R.	666	3.3	917	2.8	1,377
Japan	495	4.0	733	3.1	1,158
Eastern Europe (excluding U.S.S.R.)	330	3.3	454	2.8	682
Western Europe	1,598	4.0	2,366	3.1	3,740

[a]Projected growth rates of gross national product were developed using complex computer simulation techniques described in Chapter 16 of the Global 2000 Technical Report. These projections represent the result of applying those projected growth rates to the 1975 GNP data presented in the 1976 World Bank Atlas. Projections shown here are for medium-growth rates.

[b]Includes Puerto Rico.

[c]In most cases, gross national income growth rates were projected for groups of countries rather than for individual countries. Thus the rates attributed to individual LDCs in this table are the growth rates applicable to the group with which that country was aggregated for making projections and do not take into account country specific characteristics.

[d]Does not include Puerto Rico.

Source: Global 2000 Technical Report, Table 3-3.

TABLE 4
Per Capita GNP Estimates (1975) and Projections and Growth Rates (1985, 2000) by Major Regions and Selected Countries and Regions

(Constant 1975 U.S. dollars)

	1975	Average Annual Growth Rate, 1975–85	1985 Projections[a]	Average Annual Growth Rate, 1985–2000	2000 Projections[a]
		percent		*percent*	
WORLD	1,473	2.3	1,841	1.5	2,311
More developed countries	4,325	3.2	5,901	2.5	8,485
Less developed countries	382	2.8	501	2.1	587
MAJOR REGIONS					
Africa	405	2.2	505	1.4	620
Asia and Oceania	306	2.7	398	2.3	557
Latin America[b]	1,005	2.6	1,304	1.8	1,715
U.S.S.R. and Eastern Europe	2,591	2.4	3,279	2.1	4,472
North America, Western Europe, Japan, Australia, and New Zealand	5,431	3.4	7,597	2.6	11,117
SELECTED COUNTRIES AND REGIONS[c]					
People's Republic of China	306	2.3	384	2.3	540
India	148	1.5	171	0.8	194
Indonesia	179	4.1	268	3.1	422
Bangladesh	111	0.6	118	0.1	120
Pakistan	138	0.4	144	−0.1	142
Philippines	368	3.2	503	2.3	704
Thailand	343	3.0	460	2.2	633
South Korea	507	3.5	718	2.7	1,071
Egypt	313	2.9	416	2.2	578
Nigeria	367	3.3	507	2.2	698
Brazil	991	2.2	1,236	1.6	1,563
Mexico	1,188	2.0	1,454	1.3	1,775
United States[d]	7,066	3.3	9.756	2.5	14,212
U.S.S.R.	2,618	2.3	3,286	2.1	4,459
Japan	4,437	3.1	6,023	2.5	8,712
Eastern Europe	2,539	2.6	3,265	2.2	4,500
Western Europe	4,653	3.7	6,666	2.7	9,889

[a]The medium-series projections of gross national product and population presented in Tables 3-3 and 3-4 of the Global 2000 Technical Report were used to calculate the 1975, 1985, and 2000 per capita gross national product figures presented in this table.
[b]Includes Puerto Rico.
[c]In most cases, gross national product growth rates were projected for groups of countries rather than for individual countries. Thus, the rates attributed to individual LDCs in this table are the growth rates applicable to the group with which that country was aggregated for making projections and do not take into account country-specific characteristics.
[d]Does not include Puerto Rico.
Source: Global 2000 Technical Report, Table 3-5.

The projections indicate that most of the increase in food production will come from more intensive use of yield-enhancing, energy-intensive inputs and technologies such as fertilizer, pesticides, herbicides, and irrigation—in many cases with diminishing returns. Land under cultivation is projected to increase only 4 percent by 2000 because most good land is already being cultivated. In the early 1970s one hectare of arable land supported an average of 2.6 persons; by 2000 one hectare will have to support 4 persons. Because of this tightening land constraint, food production is not likely to increase fast enough to meet rising demands unless world agriculture becomes significantly more dependent on petroleum and petroleum-related inputs. Increased petroleum dependence also has implications for the cost of food production. After decades of generally falling prices, the real price of food is projected to increase 95 percent over the 1970–2000 period, in significant part as a result of increased petroleum dependence.[31] If energy prices in fact rise more rapidly than the projections anticipate, then the effect on food prices could be still more marked.

On the average, world food production is projected to increase more rapidly than world population, with average per capita consumption increasing about 15 percent between 1970 and 2000. Per capita consumption in the industrialized nations is projected to rise 21 percent from 1970 levels, with increases of from 40 to more than 50 percent in Japan, Eastern Europe, and the U.S.S.R., and 28 percent in the United States.* In the LDCs, however, rising food output will barely keep ahead of population growth.[32]

An increase of 9 percent in per capita food consumption is projected for the LDCs as a whole, but with enormous variations among regions and nations. The great populous countries of South Asia—expected to contain 1.3 billion people by 2000—improve hardly at all, nor do large areas of low-income North Africa and the Middle East. Per capita consumption in the sub-Saharan African LDCs will actually decline, according to the projections. The LDCs showing the greatest per capita growth (increases of about 25 percent) are concentrated in Latin America and East Asia.[33] Table 5 summarizes the projections for food production and consumption, and Table 6 and Figure 5 show per capita food consumption by regions.

The outlook for improved diets for the poorest people in the poorest LDCs is sobering. In the 1970s, consumption of calories in the LDCs averaged only 94 percent of the minimum requirements set by the U.N. Food and Agriculture Organization (FAO).† Moreover, income and

---

*"Consumption" statistics are based on the amount of food that leaves the farms and does not leave the country and therefore include transportation and processing losses. Projected increases in per capita consumption in countries like the United States, where average consumption is already at least nutritionally adequate, reflect increasing losses of food during transportation and processing and might also be accounted for by increased industrial demand for grain, especially for fermentation into fuels.

†The FAO standard indicates the *minimum* consumption that will allow normal activity and good health in adults and will permit children to reach normal body weight and intelligence in the absence of disease.

food distribution within individual LDCs is so skewed that national average caloric consumption generally must be 10–20 percent above minimum levels before the poorest are likely to be able to afford a diet that meets the FAO minimum standard. Latin America is the only major LDC region where average caloric consumption is projected to be 20 percent or more above the FAO minimum standard in the year 2000. In the other LDC regions—South, East, and Southeast Asia, poor areas of North Africa and the Middle East, and especially Central Africa, where a calamitous drop in food per capita is projected—the quantity of food available to the poorest groups of people will simply be insufficient to permit children to reach normal body weight and intelligence and to permit normal activity and good health in adults. Consumption in the LDCs of central Africa is projected to be more than 20 percent below the FAO minimum standard, assuming no recurrence of severe drought. In South Asia (primarily India, Pakistan, and Bangladesh), average caloric intake is projected to remain below the FAO minimum standard, although increasing slightly—from 12 percent below the FAO standard in the mid-1970s to about 3 percent below the standard in 2000. In East Asia, Southeast Asia, and affluent areas of North Africa and the Middle East, average per capita caloric intakes are projected to be 6-17 percent above FAO minimum requirement levels, but because the great majority of people in these regions are extremely poor, they will almost certainly continue to eat less than the minimum. The World Bank has estimated that the number of malnourished people in LDCs could rise from 400–600 million in the mid-1970s to 1.3 billion in 2000.[34]

The projected food situation has many implications for food assistance and trade. In the developing world, the need for imported food is expected to grow. The most prosperous LDCs will turn increasingly to the world commercial markets. In the poorest countries, which lack the wherewithal to buy food, requirements for international food assistance will expand. LDC exporters (especially Argentina and Thailand) are projected to enlarge food production for export because of their cost advantage over countries dependent on energy-intensive inputs. LDC grain-exporting countries, which accounted for only a little more than 10 percent of the world grain

TABLE 5
Grain Production, Consumption, and Trade, Actual and Projected,
and Percent Increase in Total Food Production and Consumption

	Grain (million metric tons)			Food (Percent increase over the 1970-2000 period)
	1969–71	1973–75	2000	
Industrialized countries				
Production	401.7	434.7	679.1	43.7
Consumption	374.3	374.6	610.8	47.4
Trade	+ 32.1	+ 61.6	+ 68.3	
United States				
Production	208.7	228.7	402.0	78.5
Consumption	169.0	158.5	272.4	51.3
Trade	+ 39.9	+ 72.9	+ 129.6	
Other developed exporters				
Production	58.6	61.2	106.1	55.6
Consumption	33.2	34.3	65.2	66.8
Trade	+ 28.4	+ 27.7	+ 40.9	
Western Europe				
Production	121.7	132.9	153.0	14.6
Consumption	144.2	151.7	213.1	31.6
Trade	− 21.8	− 19.7	− 60.1	
Japan				
Production	12.7	11.9	18.0	31.5
Consumption	27.9	30.1	60.1	92.8
Trade	− 14.4	− 19.3	− 42.1	
Centrally planned countries				
Production	401.0	439.4	722.0	74.0
Consumption	406.6	472.4	758.5	79.9
Trade	− 5.2	− 24.0	− 36.5	
Eastern Europe				
Production	72.1	89.4	140.0	83.2
Consumption	78.7	97.7	151.5	81.7
Trade	− 6.1	− 7.8	− 11.5	
U.S.S.R.				
Production	165.0	179.3	290.0	72.7
Consumption	161.0	200.7	305.0	85.9
Trade	+ 3.9	− 10.6	− 15.0	
People's Republic of China				
Production	163.9	176.9	292.0	69.0
Consumption	166.9	180.8	302.0	71.4
Trade	− 3.0	− 3.9	− 10.0	

market in 1975, are projected to capture more than 20 percent of the market by 2000. The United States is expected to continue its role as the world's principal food exporter. Moreover, as the year 2000 approaches and more marginal, weather-sensitive lands are brought into production around the world, the United States is likely to become even more of a residual world supplier than today; that is, U.S. producers will be responding to widening, weather-related swings in world production and foreign demand.[35]

Revised and updated food projections would reflect reduced estimates of future yields, increased pressure on the agricultural resource base, and several changes in national food policies.

Farmers' costs of raising—and even maintaining—yields have increased rapidly in recent years. The costs of energy-intensive, yield-enhancing inputs—fertilizer, pesticides, and fuels—have risen very rapidly throughout the world, and where these inputs are heavily used, increased applications are bringing diminishing returns. In the United States, the real cost of producing food increased roughly 10 percent in both

TABLE 5 (Cont.)

	Grain (million metric tons)			Food (Percent increase over the 1970-2000 period)
	1969–71	1973–75	2000	
Less developed countries				
Production	306.5	328.7	740.6	147.7
Consumption	326.6	355.0	772.4	142.8
Trade	− 18.5	− 29.5	− 31.8	
Exporters[a]				
Production	30.1	34.5	84.0	125.0
Consumption	18.4	21.5	36.0	58.0
Trade	+ 11.3	+ 13.1	+ 48.0	
Importers[b]				
Production	276.4	294.2	656.6	149.3
Consumption	308.2	333.5	736.4	148.9
Trade	− 29.8	− 42.6	− 79.8	
Latin America				
Production	63.8	72.0	185.9	184.4
Consumption	61.2	71.2	166.0	165.3
Trade	+ 3.2	+ 0.2	+ 19.9	
North Africa/Middle East				
Production	38.9	42.4	89.0	157.8
Consumption	49.5	54.1	123.7	167.3
Trade	− 9.1	− 13.8	− 29.7	
Other African LDCs				
Production	32.0	31.3	63.7	104.9
Consumption	33.0	33.8	63.0	96.4
Trade	− 1.0	− 2.4	+ 0.7	
South Asia				
Production	119.1	127.7	259.0	116.8
Consumption	125.3	135.1	275.7	119.4
Trade	− 6.2	− 9.3	− 16.7	
Southeast Asia				
Production	22.8	21.4	65.0	210.0
Consumption	19.3	17.9	47.0	163.6
Trade	+ 3.4	+ 3.7	+ 18.0	
East Asia				
Production	29.9	34.0	73.0	155.3
Consumption	38.3	42.9	97.0	164.9
Trade	− 8.8	− 9.7	− 24.0	
World				
Production/Consumption	1,108.0	1,202.0	2,141.7	91.0

Note: In grade figures, plus sign indicates export, minus sign indicates import.

[a]Argentina and Thailand.

[b]All others, including several countries that export in some scenarios (e.g., Brazil, Indonesia, and Colombia).

Source: Global 2000 Technical Report, Table 6-5.

1978 and 1979.[36] Other industrialized countries have experienced comparable production cost increases. Cost increases in the LDCs appear to be lower, but are still 2-3 times the annual increases of the 1960s and early 1970s. While there have been significant improvements recently in the yields of selected crops, the diminishing returns and rapidly rising costs of yield-enhancing inputs suggest that yields overall will increase more slowly than projected.

Since the food projections were made, there have been several important shifts in national food and agricultural policy concerns. In most industrialized countries, concern with protecting agricultural resources, especially soils, has increased as the resource implications of sustained

TABLE 6
Per Capita Grain Production, Consumption, and Trade, Actual and Projected,
and Percent Increase in Per Capita Total Food Production and Consumption

	Grain (kilograms per capita)			Food (Percent increase over the 1970-2000 period)
	1969–71	1973–75	2000	
Industrialized countries				
Production	573.6	592.6	769.8	18.4
Consumption	534.4	510.7	692.4	21.2
Trade	+45.8	+84.0	+77.4	
United States				
Production	1,018.6	1,079.3	1,640.3	51.1
Consumption	824.9	748.0	1,111.5	28.3
Trade	+194.7	+344.0	+528.8	
Other developed exporters				
Production	1,015.6	917.0	915.6	−11.3
Consumption	575.4	514.0	562.6	−5.7
Trade	+492.2	+415.0	+353.0	
Western Europe				
Production	364.9	388.4	394.0	1.0
Consumption	432.4	443.3	548.8	15.5
Trade	−65.4	−57.6	−154.8	
Japan				
Production	121.7	108.5	135.4	6.1
Consumption	267.5	274.4	452.3	54.2
Trade	−138.1	−175.9	−316.7	
Centrally planned countries				
Production	356.1	368.0	451.1	29.6
Consumption	361.0	395.6	473.9	35.8
Trade	−4.6	−20.1	−22.8	
Eastern Europe				
Production	574.0	693.0	921.9	53.3
Consumption	626.6	757.4	997.6	52.1
Trade	−48.6	−60.5	−75.8	
U.S.S.R.				
Production	697.6	711.2	903.2	28.1
Consumption	663.1	796.1	949.9	41.4
Trade	+16.1	−42.0	−46.7	
People's Republic of China				
Production	216.3	217.6	259.0	17.4
Consumption	220.2	222.4	267.8	19.1
Trade	−4.0	−4.8	−8.8	

production of record quantities of food here become more apparent. Debate on the 1981 U.S. farm bill, for example, will certainly include more consideration of "exporting top soil" than was foreseeable at the time the Global 2000 Study's food projections were made.[37] The heightened concern for protection of agricultural resources is leading to a search for policies that encourage improved resource management practices. Still further pressure on the resource base can be expected, however, due to rising industrial demand for grain, especially for fermentation into alcohol-based fuels. Accelerated erosion, loss of natural soil fertility and other deterioration of the agricultural resource base may have more effect in the coming years than is indicated in the Global 2000 food projections.

In the LDCs, many governments are attempting to accelerate investment in food production capacity. This policy emphasis offers important long-term benefits. Some LDC governments are intervening more frequently in domestic food markets to keep food prices low, but often at the cost of low rural incomes and slowed development

TABLE 6 (Cont.)

	Grain (kilograms per capita)			Food Percent increase over the 1970–2000 period
	1969–71	1973–75	2000	
Less developed countries				
Production	176.7	168.7	197.1	10.8
Consumption	188.3	182.2	205.5	8.6
Trade	− 10.7	− 15.1	− 8.4	
Exportersa				
Production	491.0	521.9	671.7	10.4
Consumption	300.1	325.3	287.8	− 22.6
Trade	+ 184.3	+ 198.2	+ 383.9	
Importersb				
Production	159.4	173.8	180.7	10.8
Consumption	177.7	193.6	202.7	10.8
Trade	− 17.2	− 24.1	− 21.9	
Latin America				
Production	236.1	241.0	311.4	33.7
Consumption	226.5	238.3	278.1	25.1
Trade	+ 11.8	+ 2.7	+ 33.3	
North Africa/Middle East				
Production	217.1	214.6	222.5	− 1.8
Consumption	276.2	273.8	292.8	2.2
Trade	− 50.8	− 69.8	− 70.3	
Other African LDCs				
Production	134.9	118.3	113.2	− 15.5
Consumption	139.1	127.7	112.0	− 19.1
Trade	− 4.2	− 9.1	+ 1.2	
South Asia				
Production	161.6	162.4	170.0	4.6
Consumption	170.0	171.8	181.0	5.8
Trade	− 8.4	− 11.8	− 11.0	
Southeast Asia				
Production	244.7	214.5	316.5	35.9
Consumption	207.2	182.6	228.5	14.6
Trade	+ 37.5	+ 31.9	+ 87.5	
East Asia				
Production	137.3	136.0	163.5	22.8
Consumption	176.2	171.5	217.3	27.3
Trade	− 40.4	− 38.8	− 53.8	
World				
Production/Consumption	311.5	313.6	343.2	14.5

Note: In trade figures, plus sign indicates export, minus sign indicates import.

aArgentina and Thailand.

bAll others, including several countries that export in some scenarios (e.g., Brazil, Indonesia, and Colombia).

Source: Global 2000 Technical Report, Table 6-6.

---

of agricultural production capacity.[38]

Worldwide, the use of yield-enhancing inputs is likely to be less, and soil deterioration greater, than expected. As a result, revised food projections would show a tighter food future—somewhat less production and somewhat higher prices—than indicated in the Global 2000 projections.

Fisheries

Fish is an important component of the world's diet and has sometimes been put forth as a possible partial solution to world food shortages. Unfortunately, the world harvest of fish is expected to rise little, if at all, by the year 2000.* The world catch of naturally produced fish leveled off in the 1970s at about 70 million metric tons a year

---

*The food projections assumed that the world fish catch would increase at essentially the same rate as population and are therefore likely to prove too optimistic on this point. (See Chapters 6, 14, and 18 of the Global 2000 Technical Report for further discussion of this point.)

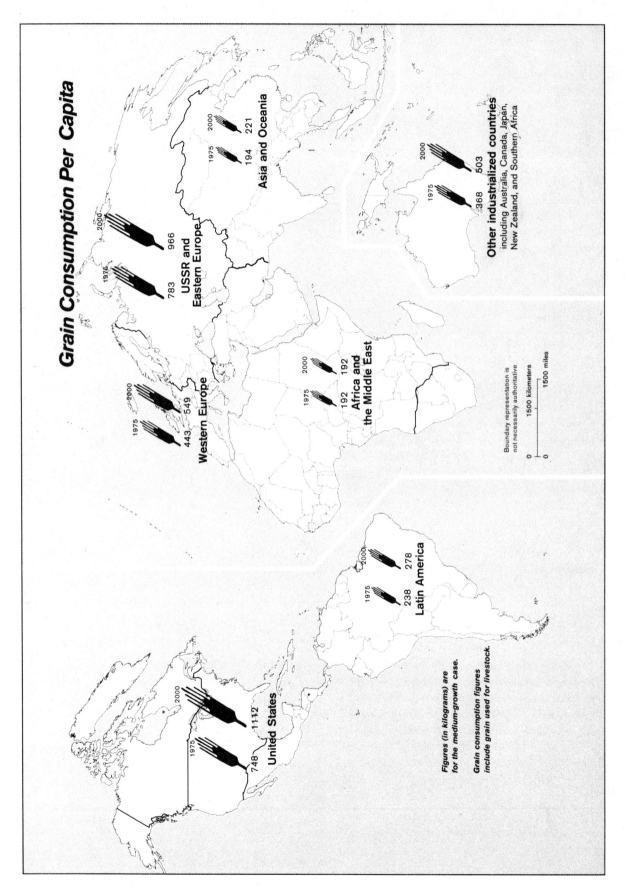

Figure 5. Per capita grain consumption, by regions, 1975 and 2000.

(60 million metric tons for marine fisheries, 10 million metric tons for freshwater species). Harvests of traditional fisheries are not likely to increase on a sustained basis, and indeed to maintain them will take good management and improved protection of the marine environment. Some potential for greater harvests comes from aquaculture and from nontraditional marine species, such as Antarctic krill, that are little used at present for direct human consumption.[39]

Traditional freshwater and marine species might be augmented in some areas by means of aquaculture. The 1976 FAO World Conference on Aquaculture concluded that a five- to tenfold increase in production from aquaculture would be possible by 2000, given adequate financial and technical support. (Aquaculture contributed an estimated 6 million metric tons to the world's total catch in 1975.) However, limited investment and technical support, as well as increasing pollution of freshwater ponds and coastal water, are likely to be a serious impediment to such growth.[40]

While fish is not a solution to the world needs for calories, fish does provide an important source of protein. The 70 million metric tons caught and raised in 1975 is roughly equivalent to 14 million metric tons of protein, enough to supply 27 percent of the minimum protein requirements of 4 billion people. (Actually since more than one-third of the fish harvest is used for animal feed, not food for humans, the contribution of fish to human needs for protein is lower than these figures suggest.[41]) A harvest of about 115 million metric tons would be required to supply 27 percent of the protein needs of 6.35 billion people in 2000. Even assuming that the catch of marine and freshwater fish rises to the unlikely level of 100 million metric tons annually, and that yields from aquaculture double, rising to 12 million tons, the hypothetical total of 112 metric tons would not provide as much protein per capita as the catch of the mid-1970s. Thus, on a per capita basis, fish may well contribute less to the world's nutrition in 2000 than today.

Updated fisheries projections would show little change from the Global 2000 Study projections. FAO fisheries statistics are now available for 1978 and show a world catch of 72.4 million metric tons. (The FAO statistics for the 1970-78 period have been revised downward somewhat to reflect improved data on the catch of the People's Republic of China.) While there has been some slight recovery of the anchovy and menhaden fisheries, traditional species continue to show signs of heavy pressure. As indicated in the Global 2000 projections, the catch of nontraditional species is filling in to some extent. Perhaps the biggest change in updated fisheries projections would stem from a careful analysis of the effects of the large increase in oil prices that occurred in 1979. Scattered observations suggest that fishing fleets throughout the world are being adversely affected except where governments are keeping oil prices to fishing boats artificially low.[42]

Forests

If present trends continue, both forest cover and growing stocks of commercial-size wood in the less developed regions (Latin America, Africa, Asia, and Oceania) will decline 40 percent by 2000. In the industrialized regions (Europe,

TABLE 7
Estimates of World Forest Resources, 1978 and 2000

	Closed Forest[a] (millions of hectares)		Growing Stock (billions cu m overbark)	
	1978	2000	1978	2000
U.S.S.R.	785	775	79	77
Europe	140	150	15	13
North America	470	464	58	55
Japan, Australia, New Zealand	69	68	4	4
Subtotal	1,464	1,457	156	149
Latin America	550	329	94	54
Africa	188	150	39	31
Asia and Pacific LDCs	361	181	38	19
Subtotal (LDCs)	1,099	660	171	104
Total (world)	2,563	2,117	327	253

	Growing Stock per Capita (cu m biomass)	
Industrial countries	142	114
LDCs	57	21
Global	76	40

[a]Closed forests are relatively dense and productive forests. They are defined variously in different parts of the world. For further details, see Global 2000 Technical Report, footnote, p. 117.

Source: Global 2000 Technical Report, Table 13-29.

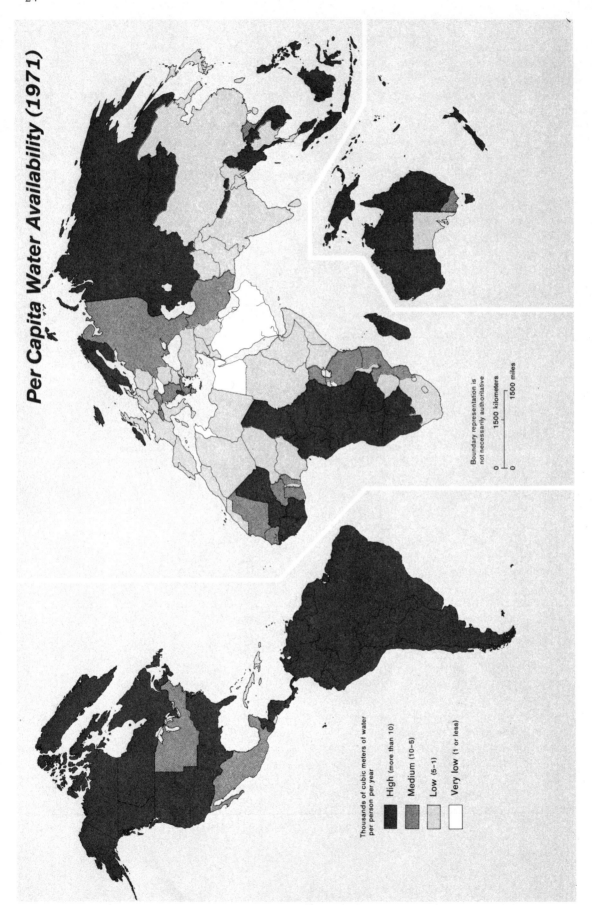

Per Capita Water Availability (1971)

Thousands of cubic meters of water
per person per year

High (more than 10)
Medium (10–5)
Low (5–1)
Very low (1 or less)

Boundary representation is
not necessarily authoritative

0   1500 kilometers
0   1500 miles

Figure 6. Per capita water availability, 1971.

25

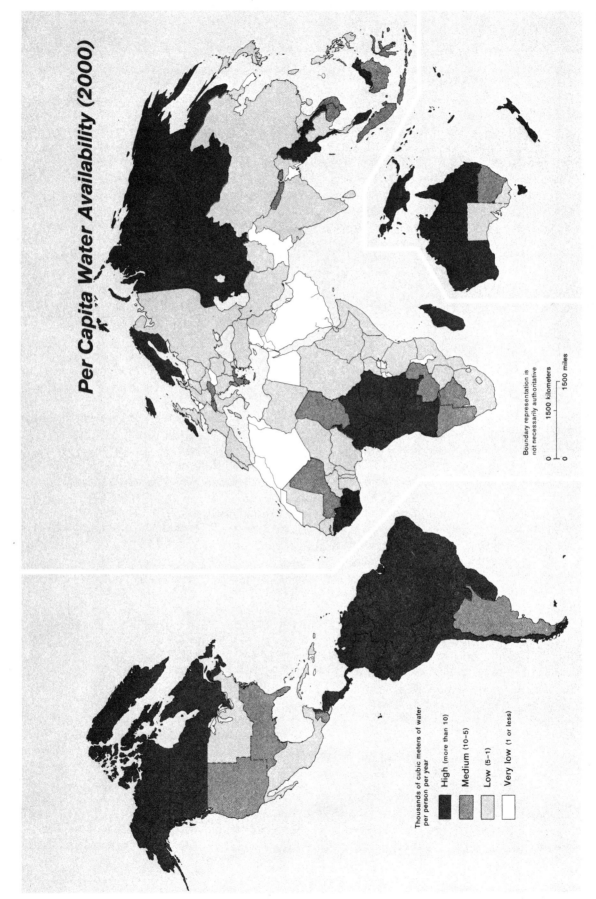

Figure 7. Projected per capita water availability, 2000.

the U.S.S.R., North America, Japan, Australia, New Zealand) forests will decline only 0.5 percent and growing stock about 5 percent. Growing stock per capita is expected to decline 47 percent worldwide and 63 percent in LDCs.[43] Table 7 shows projected forest cover and growing stocks by region for 1978 and 2000.

Deforestation is projected to continue until about 2020, when the total world forest area will stabilize at about 1.8 billion hectares. Most of the loss will occur in the tropical forests of the developing world. About 1.45 billion hectares of forest in the industrialized nations has already stabilized and about 0.37 billion hectares of forest in the LDCs is physically or economically inaccessible. By 2020, virtually all of the physically accessible forest in the LDCs is expected to have been cut.[44]

The real prices of wood products—fuelwood, sawn lumber, wood panels, paper, wood-based chemicals, and so on—are expected to rise considerably as GNP (and thus also demand) rises and world supplies tighten. In the industrialized nations, the effects may be disruptive, but not catastrophic. In the less developed countries, however, 90 percent of wood consumption goes for cooking and heating, and wood is a necessity of life. Loss of woodlands will force people in many LDCs to pay steeply rising prices for fuelwood and charcoal or to spend much more effort collecting wood—or else to do without.[45]

Updated forest projections would present much the same picture as the Global 2000 Study projections. The rapid increase in the price of crude oil will probably limit the penetration of kerosene sales into areas now depending on fuelwood and dung and, as a result, demand for fuelwood may be somewhat higher than expected. Some replanting of cut tropical areas is occurring, but only at low rates similar to those assumed in the Global 2000 Study projections. Perhaps the most encouraging developments are those associated with heightened international awareness of the seriousness of current trends in world forests.[46]

Water

The Global 2000 Study population, GNP, and resource projections all imply rapidly increasing demands for fresh water.[47] Increases of at least 200-300 percent in world water withdrawals are expected over the 1975-2000 period. By far the largest part of the increase is for irrigation. The United Nations has estimated that water needed for irrigation, which accounted for 70 percent of human uses of water in 1967, would double by 2000. Moreover, irrigation is a highly consumptive use, that is, much of the water withdrawn for this purpose is not available for immediate reuse because it evaporates, is transpired by plants, or becomes salinated.[48]

Regional water shortages and deterioration of water quality, already serious in many parts of the world, are likely to become worse by 2000. Estimates of per capita water availability for 1971 and 2000, based on population growth alone, *without allowance for other causes of increased demand,* are shown in Figures 6 and 7. As indicated in these maps, population growth alone will cause demands for water at least to double relative to 1971 in nearly half the countries of the world. Still greater increases would be needed to improve standards of living.[49]

Much of the increased demand for water will be in the LDCs of Africa, South Asia, the Middle East, and Latin America, where in many areas fresh water for human consumption and irrigation is already in short supply. Although the data are sketchy, it is known that several nations in these areas will be approaching their maximum developable water supply by 2000, and that it will be quite expensive to develop the water remaining. Moreover, many LDCs will also suffer destabilization of water supplies following extensive loss of forests. In the industrialized countries competition among different uses of water—for increasing food production, new energy systems (such as production of synthetic fuels from coal and shale), increasing power generation, expanding food production, and increasing needs of other industry—will aggravate water shortages in many areas.[50]

Updated water projections would present essentially the same picture. The only significant change that has occurred since the projections were developed is that the price of energy (especially oil) has increased markedly. Increased energy costs will adversely affect the economics of many water development projects, and may reduce the amount of water available for a variety of uses. Irrigation, which usually requires large amounts of energy for pumping, may be particularly affected.

Nonfuel Minerals

The trends for nonfuel minerals, like those for the other resources considered in the Global 2000 Study, show steady increases in demand and consumption. The global demand for and consumption of most major nonfuel mineral commodities is projected to increase 3-5 percent annually, slightly more than doubling by 2000. Consumption of all major steelmaking mineral commodities is projected to increase at least 3 percent annually. Consumption of all mineral commodities for fertilizer production is projected to grow at more than 3 percent annually, with consumption of phosphate rock growing at 5.2 percent per year—the highest growth rate projected for any of the major nonfuel mineral commodities. The nonferrous metals show widely varying projected growth rates; the growth rate for aluminum, 4.3 percent per year, is the largest.[51]

The projections suggest that the LDC's share of nonfuel mineral use will increase only modestly. Over the 1971-75 period, Latin America, Africa, and Asia used 7 percent of the world's aluminum production, 9 percent of the copper, and 12 percent of the iron ore. The three-quarters of the world's population living in these regions in 2000 are projected to use only 8 percent of aluminum production, 13 percent of copper production, and 17 percent of iron ore production. The one-quarter of the world's population that inhabits industrial countries is projected to continue absorbing more than three-fourths of the world's nonfuel minerals production.[52] Figure 8 shows the geographic distribution of per capita consumption of nonfuel minerals for 1975 and 2000.

The projections point to no mineral exhaustion problems but, as indicated in Table 8, further discoveries and investments will be needed to maintain reserves and production of several mineral commodities at desirable levels. In most cases, however, the resource potential is still large (see Table 9), especially for low grade ores.[53]

Updated nonfuel minerals projections would need to give further attention to two factors affecting investment in mining. One is the shift over the past decade in investment in extraction and processing away from the developing countries toward industrialized countries (although this

trend may now be reversing). The other factor is the rapid increase in energy prices. Production of many nonfuel minerals is highly energy-intensive, and the recent and projected increases in oil prices can be expected to slow the expansion of these mineral supplies.[54]

Energy

The Global 2000 Study's energy projections show no early relief from the world's energy problems. The projections point out that petroleum production capacity is not increasing as rapidly as demand. Furthermore, the rate at which petroleum reserves are being added per unit of exploratory effort appears to be falling. Engineering and geological considerations suggest that world petroleum production will peak before the end of the century. Political and economic decisions in the OPEC countries could cause oil production to level off even before technological constraints come into play. A world transition away from petroleum dependence must take place, but there is still much uncertainty as to how this transition will occur. In the face of this uncertainty, it was not possible at the time the Global 2000 energy projections were made—late 1977—for the Department of Energy (DOE) to develop meaningful energy projections beyond 1990.[55] Updated DOE analyses, discussed at the end of this section, extend the global energy projections available from the U.S. Government to 1995.

DOE projections prepared for the Study show large increases in demand for all commercial sources over the 1975-90 period (see Table 10). World energy demand is projected to increase 58 percent, reaching 384 quads (quadrillion British thermal units) by 1990. Nuclear and hydro sources (primarily nuclear) increase most rapidly (226 percent by 1990), followed by oil (58 percent), natural gas (43 percent), and coal (13 percent). Oil is projected to remain the world's leading energy source, providing 46-47 percent of the world's total energy through 1990, assuming that the real price of oil on the international market increases 65 percent over the 1975-90 period. The energy projections indicate that there is considerable potential for reductions in energy consumption.[56]

Per capita energy consumption is projected to increase everywhere. The largest increase—72 percent over the 1975-90 period—is in industrialized countries other than the United States. The

28

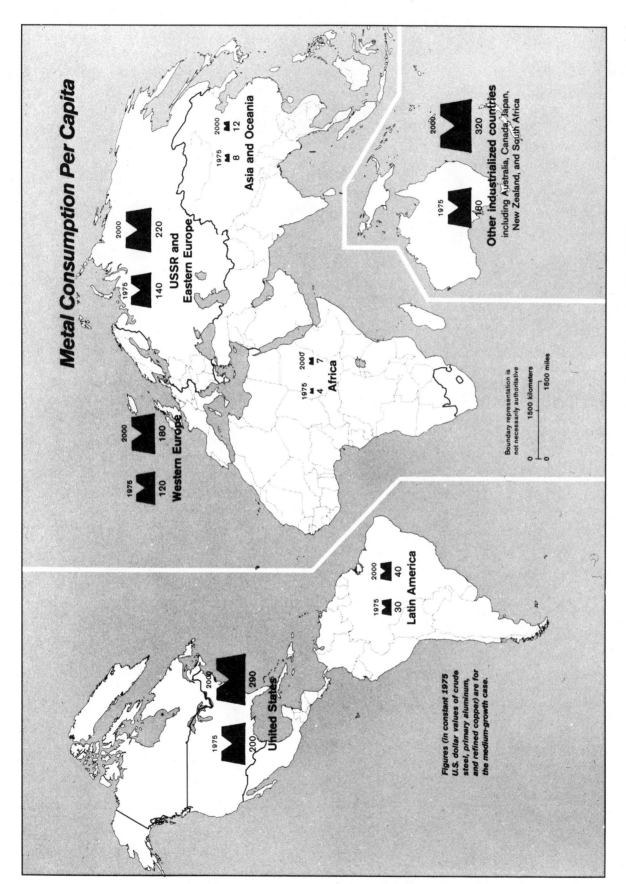

Figure 8. Distribution of per capita consumption of nonfuel minerals, 1975 and 2000.

TABLE 8
**Life Expectancies of 1976 World Reserves of Selected Mineral Commodities
at Two Different Rates of Demand**

	1976 Reserves	1976 Primary Demand	Projected Demand Growth Rate	Life Expectancy in Years[a]	
				Static at 1976 Level	Growing at Projected Rates
			percent		
Fluorine (*million short tons*)	37	2.1	4.58	18	13
Silver (*million troy ounces*)	6,100	305	2.33	20	17
Zinc (*million short tons*)	166	6.4	3.05	26	19
Mercury (*thousand flasks*)	5,210	239	0.50	22	21
Sulfur (*million long tons*)	1,700	50	3.16	34	23
Lead (*million short tons*)	136	3.7	3.14	37	25
Tungsten (*million pounds*)	4,200	81	3.26	52	31
Tin (*thousand metric tons*)	10,000	241	2.05	41	31
Copper (*million short tons*)	503	8.0	2.94	63	36
Nickel (*million short tons*)	60	0.7	2.94	86	43
Platinum (*million troy ounces*)	297	2.7	3.75	110	44
Phosphate rock (*million metric tons*)	25,732	107	5.17	240	51
Manganese (*million short tons*)	1,800	11.0	3.36	164	56
Iron in ore (*billion short tons*)	103	0.6	2.95	172	62
Aluminum in bauxite (*million short tons*)	5,610	18	4.29	312	63
Chromium (*million short tons*)	829	2.2	3.27	377	80
Potash (*million short tons*)	12,230	26	3.27	470	86

Note: Corresponding data for helium and industrial diamonds not available.
[a]Assumes no increase to 1976 reserves.
Source: After Global 2000 Technical Report, Table 12-4, but with updated and corrected entries. Updated reserves and demand data from U.S. Bureau of Mines, *Mineral Trends and Forecasts*, 1979. Projected demand growth rates are from Global 2000 Technical Report, Table 12-2.

smallest increase, 12 percent, is in the centrally planned economies of Eastern Europe. The percentage increases for the United States and for the LDCs are the same—27 percent—but actual per capita energy consumption is very different. By 2000, U.S. per capita energy consumption is projected to be about 422 million Btu (British thermal units) annually. In the LDCs, it will be only 14 million Btu, up from 11 million in 1975[57] (see Table 11 and Figure 9).

While prices for oil and other commercial energy sources are rising, fuelwood—the poor person's oil—is expected to become far less available than it is today. The FAO has estimated that the demand for fuelwood in LDCs will increase at 2.2 percent per year, leading to local fuelwood shortages in 1994 totaling 650 million cubic meters— approximately 25 percent of the projected need. Scarcities are now local but expanding. In the arid Sahel of Africa, fuelwood gathering has become a full-time job requiring in some places 360 person-days of work per household each year. When demand is concentrated in cities, surrounding areas have already become barren for considerable distances—50 to 100 kilometers in some places. Urban families, too far from collectible wood, spend 20 to 30 percent of their income on wood in some West African cities.[58]

The projected shortfall of fuelwood implies that fuel consumption for essential uses will be reduced, deforestation expanded, wood prices increased, and growing amounts of dung and crop residues shifted from the field to the cooking fire. No explicit projections of dung and crop residue combustion could be made for the Study, but it is known that a shift toward burning these organic materials is already well advanced in the Himalayan hills, in the treeless Ganges plain of India, in other parts of Asia, and in the Andean region of South America. The FAO reports that in 1970 India burned 68 million tons of cow dung and 39 million tons of vegetable waste, accounting for roughly a third of the nation's total noncommercial energy consumption that year. Worldwide, an estimated 150-400 million tons of dung are burned annually for fuel.[59]

30

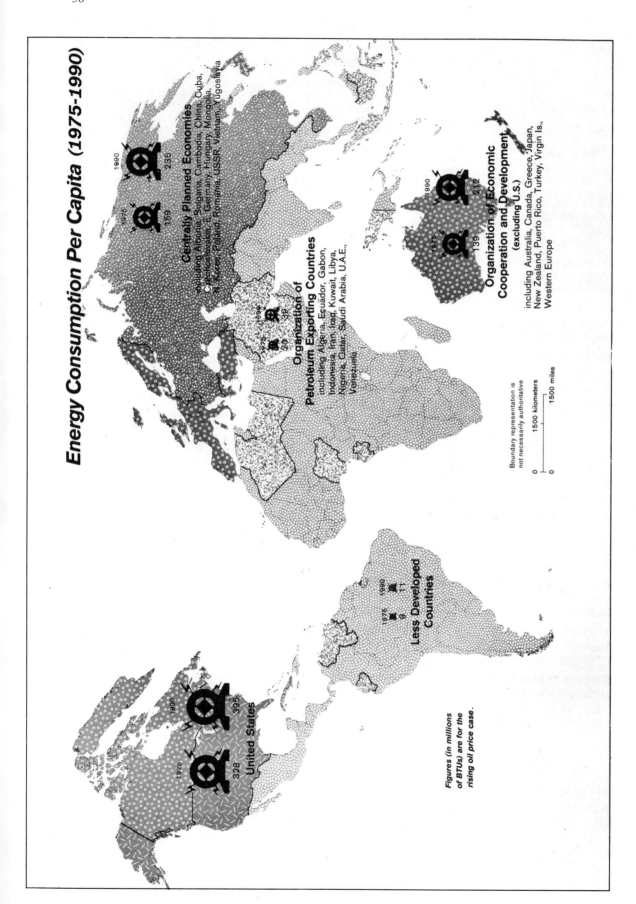

Figure 9. Energy consumption per capita, 1975–90.

TABLE 9
World Production and Reserves in 1977 (Estimated), Other Resources in 1973–77 (as Data Available), Resource Potential, and Resource Base of 17 Elements

(Millions of metric tons)

	Production	Reserves	Other Resources	Resource Potential (Recoverable)	Resource Base (Crustal Mass)
Aluminum	17[a]	5,200[a]	2,800[a]	3,519,000	1,990,000,000,000
Iron	495[b]	93,100	143,000[c]	2,035,000	1,392,000,000,000
Potassium	22	9,960	103,000	n.a.	408,000,000,000
Manganese	10[d]	2,200	1,100[e]	42,000	31,200,000,000
Phosphorus	14[f]	3,400[f]	12,000[f]	51,000	28,800,000,000
Fluorine	2[g]	72	270	20,000	10,800,000,000
Sulfur	52	1,700	3,800[h]		9,600,000,000
Chromium	3[i]	780[i]	6,000[i]	3,260	2,600,000,000
Zinc	6	159	4,000	3,400	2,250,000,000
Nickel	0.7	54	103[e]	2,590	2,130,000,000
Copper	8	456	1,770[j]	2,120	1,510,000,000
Lead	4	123	1,250	550	290,000,000
Tin	0.2	10	27	68	40,800,000
Tungsten	0.04	1.8	3.4	51	26,400,000
Mercury	0.008	0.2	0.4	3.4	2,100,000
Silver	0.010	0.2	0.5	2.8	1,800,000
Platinum group[k]	0.0002	0.02	0.05[l]	1.2[m]	1,100,000

[a]In bauxite, dry basis, assumed to average 21 percent recoverable aluminum.

[b]In ore and concentrates assumed to average 58 percent recoverable iron.

[c]In ore and concentrates assumed to average 26 percent recoverable iron.

[d]In ore and concentrates assumed to average 40 percent manganese.

[e]Excludes metal in deep-sea nodules and, in the case of nickel, unidentified resources.

[f]In phosphate rock ore and concentrates assumed to average 13 percent phosphorus.

[g]In fluorspar and phosphate rock ore and concentrates assumed to average 44 percent fluorine.

[h]Excludes unidentified sulfur resources, enormous quantities of sulfur in gypsum and anhydrite, and some 600 billion tons of sulfur in coal, oil shale, and in shale that is rich in organic matter.

[i]In ore and concentrates assumed to average 32 percent chromium.

[j]Includes 690 million tons in deep-sea nodules.

[k]Platinum, palladium, iridium, cesium, rhodium, and ruthenium.

[l]Approximate midpoint of estimated range of 0.03–0.06 million metric tons.

[m]Platinum only.

Source: Global 2000 Technical Report, Table 12-7.

TABLE 10
Global Primary[a] Energy Use, 1975 and 1990, by Energy Type

	1975		1990		Percent Increase (1975-90)	Average Annual Percent Increase
	10^{15} Btu	Percent of Total	10^{15} Btu[b]	Percent of Total		
Oil	113	46	179	47	58	3.1
Coal	68	28	77	20	13	0.8
Natural gas	46	19	66	17	43	2.4
Nuclear and hydro	19	8[c]	62	16[c]	226	7.9
Solar (other than conservation/ and hydro)[d]	—	—	—	—	—	—
Total	246	100	384	100	56	3.0

[a]All of the nuclear and much of the coal primary (i.e., input) energy is used thermally to generate electricity. In the process, approximately two-thirds of the primary energy is lost as waste heat. The figures given here are primary energy.

[b]The conversions from the DOE projections in Table 10-8 were made as follows: *Oil* 84.8 × 10^6 bbl/day × 365 days × 5.8 × 10^6 Btu/bbl = 179 × 10^6 Btu. *Coal:* 5,424 × 10^6 short tons/yr × 14.1 × 10^6 Btu/short ton [DOE figure for world average grade coal] = 77 × 10^{15} Btu. *Natural gas:* 64.4 × 10^{12}ft³/yr × 1,032 Btu/ft³ = 66 × 10^{15} Btu. *Nuclear and Hydro:* 6,009 × 10^{12} Wh [output]/yr × 3,412 Btu/Wh × 3 input Btu/output Btu = 62 × 10^{12} Btu.

[c]After deductions for lost (waste) heat (see note a), the corresponding figures for output energy are 2.7 percent in 1975 and 6.0 in 1990.

[d]The IIES projection model is able to include solar only as conservation or hydro.

Source: Global 2000 Technical Report, Table 13-32.

TABLE 11
Per Capita Global Primary Energy Use, Annually, 1975 and 1990

	1975		1990			
	10^6 Btu	Percent of World Average	10^6 Btu	Percent of World Average	Percent Increase (1975-90)	Average Annual Percent Increase
United States	332	553	422	586	27	1.6
Other industrialized countries	136	227	234	325	72	3.6
Less developed countries[a]	11	18	14	19	27	1.6
Centrally planned economies	58	97	65	90	12	0.8
World	60	100	72	100	20	1.2

[a]Since population projections were not made separately for the OPEC countries, those countries have been included here in LDC category.

Source: Global 2000 Technical Report, Table 13-34.

Updated energy projections have been developed by the Department of Energy based on new price scenarios that include the rapid 1979 increase in the price of crude oil. The new price scenarios are not markedly different from the earlier estimates for the 1990s. The new medium-scenario price for 1995 is $40 per barrel (in 1979 dollars), which is about 10 percent higher than the $36 price (1979 dollars) implied by the earlier scenario. However, the prices for the early 1980s are almost 100 percent higher than those in the projections made by DOE in late 1977 for the Study.[60] The sudden large increase in oil prices of 1979 is likely to have a more disruptive effect on other sectors than would the gradual increase assumed in the Global 2000 Study projections.

DOE's new projections differ in several ways from those reported in this Study. Using the higher prices, additional data, and a modified model, DOE is now able to project supply and demand for an additional five years, to 1995. Demand is projected to be lower because of the higher prices and also because of reduced estimates of economic growth. Coal is projected to provide a somewhat larger share of the total energy supply. The nuclear projections for the OECD countries are lower, reflecting revised estimates of the speed at which new nuclear plants will be built. Updated estimates of OPEC maximum production are lower than earlier estimates, reflecting trends toward resource conservation by the OPEC nations. The higher oil prices will encourage the adoption of alternative fuels and technologies, including solar technology and conservation measures.[61]

Environmental Consequences

The population, income, and resource projections all imply significant consequences for the quality of the world environment. Virtually every aspect of the earth's ecosystems and resource base will be affected.[62]

Impacts on Agriculture

Perhaps the most serious environmental development will be an accelerating deterioration and loss of the resources essential for agriculture. This overall development includes soil erosion; loss of nutrients and compaction of soils; increasing salinization of both irrigated land and water used for irrigation; loss of high-quality cropland to urban development; crop damage due to increasing air and water pollution; extinction of local and wild crop strains needed by plant breeders for improving cultivated varieties; and more frequent and more severe regional water shortages—especially where energy and industrial developments compete for water supplies, or where forest losses are heavy and the earth can no longer absorb, store, and regulate the discharge of water.

Deterioration of soils is occurring rapidly in LDCs, with the spread of desert-like conditions in drier regions, and heavy erosion in more humid areas. Present global losses to desertification are estimated at around 6 million hectares a year (an area about the size of Maine), including 3.2 million hectares of rangeland, 2.5 million hectares of rainfed cropland, and 125 thousand hectares of irrigated farmland. Desertification does not necessarily mean the creation of Sahara-like sand deserts, but rather it includes a variety of ecological changes that destroy the cover of vegetation and fertile soil in the earth's drier regions, rendering the land useless for range or crops. Principal direct causes are overgrazing, destructive cropping practices, and use of woody plants for fuel.

At presently estimated rates of desertification, the world's desert areas (now some 800 million hectares) would expand almost 20 percent by 2000. But there is reason to expect that losses to desertification will accelerate, as increasing numbers of people in the world's drier regions put more pressures on the land to meet their needs for livestock range, cropland, and fuelwood. The United Nations has identified about 2 billion hectares of lands (Figure 10) where the risk of desertification is "high" or "very high." These lands at risk total about two and one-half times the area now classified as desert.

Although soil loss and deterioration are especially serious in many LDCs, they are also affecting agricultural prospects in industrialized nations. Present rates of soil loss in many industrialized nations cannot be sustained without serious implications for crop production. In the United States, for example, the Soil Conservation Service, looking at wind and water erosion of U.S. soils, has concluded that to sustain crop production indefinitely at even present levels, soil losses must be cut in half.

The outlook for making such gains in the United States and elsewhere is not good. The food and forestry projections imply increasing pressures on soils throughout the world. Losses due to improper irrigation, reduced fallow periods, cultivation of steep and marginal lands, and reduced vegetative cover can be expected to accelerate, especially in North and Central Africa, the humid and high-altitude portions of Latin America, and much of South Asia. In addition, the increased burning of dung and crop wastes for domestic fuel will deprive the soil of nutrients and degrade the soil's ability to hold moisture by reducing its organic content. For the world's poor, these organic materials are often the only source of the nutrients needed to maintain the productivity of farmlands. It is the poorest people—those least able to afford chemical fertilizers—who are being forced to burn their organic fertilizers. These

nutrients will be urgently needed for food production in the years ahead, since by 2000 the world's croplands will have to feed half again as many people as in 1975.[63] In the industrialized regions, increasing use of chemical fertilizers, high-yield plant varieties, irrigation water, and herbicides and pesticides have so far compensated for basic declines in soil conditions. However, heavy dependence on chemical fertilizers also leads to losses of soil organic matter, reducing the capacity of the soil to retain moisture.

Damage and loss of irrigated lands are especially significant because these lands have yields far above average. Furthermore, as the amount of arable land per capita declines over the next two decades, irrigated lands will be counted upon increasingly to raise per capita food availability. As of 1975, 230 million hectares—15 percent of the world's arable area—were being irrigated; an additional 50 million hectares are expected to be irrigated by 1990. Unfortunately there is great difficulty in maintaining the productivity of irrigated lands. About half of the world's irrigated land has already been damaged to some degree by salinity, alkalinity, and waterlogging, and much of the additional land expected to be irrigated by 1990 is highly vulnerable to irrigation-related damage.

Environmental problems of irrigation exist in industrialized countries (for example, in the San Joaquin Valley in California) as well as in LDCs (as in Pakistan, where three-quarters of the irrigated lands are damaged). It is possible, but slow and costly, to restore damaged lands. Prevention requires careful consideration of soils and attention to drainage, maintenance, and appropriate water-saving designs.

Loss of good cropland to urban encroachment is another problem affecting all countries. Cities and industries are often located on a nation's best agricultural land—rich, well-watered alluvial soils in gently sloping river valleys. In the industrialized countries that are members of the OECD, the amount of land devoted to urban uses has been increasing twice as fast as population. The limited data available for LDCs point to similar trends. In Egypt, for example, despite efforts to open new lands to agriculture, the total area of irrigated farmland has remained almost unchanged in the past two decades. As fast as additional acres are irrigated with water from the

34

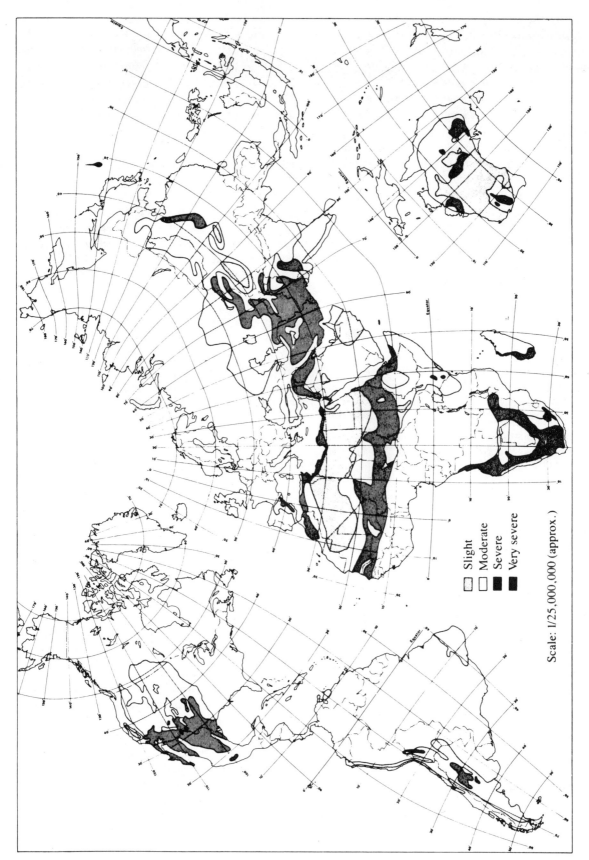

Scale: 1/25,000,000 (approx.)

Slight
Moderate
Severe
Very severe

Figure 10. Desertification map (*U.N. Desertification Conference, 1977*).

Aswan Dam, old producing lands on the Nile are converted to urban uses.

The rising yields assumed by the Global 2000 food projections depend on wider adoption of existing high-yield agricultural technology and on accelerating use of fertilizers, irrigation, pesticides, and herbicides. These yield-enhancing inputs, projected to more than double in use worldwide and to quadruple in LDCs, are heavily dependent on fossil fuels. Even now, a rapid escalation of fossil fuel prices or a sudden interruption of supply could severely disturb world agricultural production, raise food prices, and deprive larger numbers of people of adequate food. As agriculture becomes still more dependent on energy-intensive inputs, the potential for disruption will be even greater.

Accelerating use of pesticides is expected to raise crop yields quickly and substantially, especially in LDCs. Yet, many of these chemicals produce a wide range of serious environmental consequences, some of which adversely affect agricultural production. Destruction of pest predator populations and the increasing resistance of pests to heavily used pesticides have already proved to be significant agricultural problems. On California farms, for example, 17 of 25 major agricultural pests are now resistant to one or more types of pesticides, and the populations of pest predators have been severely reduced. Many millions of dollars in crop damage are now caused annually in California by resistant pests whose natural predators have been destroyed.

Crop yields are expected to be increased significantly by much wider use of high-yield strains of grains. Unfortunately, large monocultures of genetically identical crops pose increased risks of catastrophic loss from insect attacks or crop epidemics. The corn blight that struck the U.S. corn belt in 1970 provided a clear illustration of the vulnerability of genetically identical monocultures.

Impacts on Water Resources

The quality of the world's water resources is virtually certain to suffer from the changes taking place between now and the year 2000. Water pollution from heavy application of pesticides will cause increasing difficulties. In the industrialized countries, shifts from widespread use of long-lived chemicals such as DDT are now underway, but in the LDCs—where the largest increases in agricultural chemical use is projected—it is likely that the persistent pesticides will continue to be used. Pesticide use in LDCs is expected to at least quadruple over the 1975–2000 period (a sixfold increase is possible if recent rates of increase continue). Pollution from the persistent pesticides in irrigation canals, ponds, and rice paddies is already a worrisome problem. Farmers in some parts of Asia are reluctant to stock paddies and ponds because fish are being killed by pesticides. This means a serious loss of high-quality protein for the diets of rural families.

In addition to the potential impacts on soils discussed above, irrigation adversely affects water quality by adding salt to the water returning to streams and rivers. Downstream from extensive irrigation projects the water may become too saline for further use, unless expensive desalinization measures are undertaken. As the use of water for irrigation increases, water salinity problems are certain to increase as well.

Water pollution in LDCs is likely to worsen as the urban population soars and industry expands. Already the waters below many LDC cities are heavily polluted with sewage and wastes from pulp and paper mills, tanneries, slaughterhouses, oil refineries, and chemical plants.

River basin development that combines flood control, generation of electricity, and irrigation is likely to increase in many less developed regions, where most of the world's untapped hydropower potential lies. While providing many benefits, large-scale dams and irrigation projects can also cause highly adverse changes in both freshwater and coastal ecosystems, creating health problems (including schistosomiasis, river blindness, malaria), inundating valuable lands, and displacing populations. In addition, if erosion in the watersheds of these projects is not controlled, siltation and buildup of sediments may greatly reduce the useful life of the projects.

Virtually all of the Global 2000 Study's projections point to increasing destruction or pollution of coastal ecosystems, a resource on which the commercially important fisheries of the world depend heavily. It is estimated that 60-80 percent of commercially valuable marine fishery species use estuaries, salt marshes, or mangrove swamps for habitat at some point in their life cycle. Reef habitats also provide food and shelter for large numbers of fish and invertebrate species. Rapidly expanding cities and industry are likely to claim coastal wetland areas for development; and increasing coastal pollution from agriculture, industry, logging, water resources development, energy systems, and coastal communities is anticipated in many areas.

Impacts of Forest Losses

The projected rapid, widespread loss of tropical forests will have severe adverse effects on water and other resources. Deforestation—especially in South Asia, the Amazon basin, and central Africa—will destabilize water flows, leading to siltation of streams, reservoirs behind hydroelectric dams, and irrigation works, to depletion of ground water, to intensified flooding, and to aggravated water shortages during dry periods. In South and Southeast Asia approximately one billion people live in heavily farmed alluvial basins and valleys that depend on forested mountain watersheds for their water. If present trends continue, forests in these regions will be reduced by about half in 2000, and erosion, siltation, and erratic streamflows will seriously affect food production.

In many tropical forests, the soils, land forms, temperatures, patterns of rainfall, and distribution of nutrients are in precarious balance. When these forests are disturbed by extensive cutting, neither trees nor productive grasses will grow again. Even in less fragile tropical forests, the great diversity of species is lost after extensive cutting.

Impacts on the World's Atmosphere and Climate

Among the emerging environmental stresses are some that affect the chemical and physical nature of the atmosphere. Several are recognized as problems; others are more conjectural but nevertheless of concern.

Quantitative projections of urban air quality around the world are not possible with the data and models now available, but further pollution in LDCs and some industrial nations is virtually certain to occur under present policies and practices. In LDC cities, industrial growth projected for the next 20 years is likely to worsen air quality. Even now, observations in scattered LDC cities show levels of sulfur dioxide, particulates, nitrogen dioxide, and carbon monoxide far above levels considered safe by the World Health Organization. In some cities, such as Bombay and Caracas, recent rapid increases in the numbers of cars and trucks have aggravated air pollution.

Despite recent progress in reducing various types of air pollution in many industrialized countries, air quality there is likely to worsen as increased amounts of fossil fuels, especially coal, are burned. Emissions of sulfur and nitrogen oxides are particularly troubling because they combine with water vapor in the atmosphere to form acid rain or produce other acid deposition. In large areas of Norway, Sweden, southern Canada, and the eastern United States, the pH value of rainfall has dropped from 5.7 to below 4.5, well into the acidic range. Also, rainfall has almost certainly become more acid in parts of Germany, Eastern Europe, and the U.S.S.R., although available data are incomplete.

The effects of acid rain are not yet fully understood, but damage has already been observed in lakes, forests, soils, crops, nitrogen-fixing plants, and building materials. Damage to lakes has been studied most extensively. For example, of 1,500 lakes in southern Norway with a pH below 4.3, 70 percent had no fish. Similar damage has been observed in the Adirondack Mountains of New York and in parts of Canada. River fish are also severely affected. In the last 20 years, first salmon and then trout disappeared in many Norwegian rivers as acidity increased.

Another environmental problem related to the combustion of fossil fuels (and perhaps also to the global loss of forests and soil humus) is the increasing concentration of carbon dioxide in the earth's atmosphere. Rising CO_2 concentrations are of concern because of their potential for causing a warming of the earth. Scientific opinion differs on the possible consequences, but a widely held view is that highly disruptive effects on world agriculture could occur before the middle of the twenty-first century. The CO_2 content of the world's atmosphere has increased about 15 percent in the last century and by 2000 is expected to be nearly a third higher than preindustrial levels. If the projected rates of increase in fossil fuel combustion (about 2 percent per year) were to continue, a doubling of the CO_2 content of the atmosphere could be expected after the middle of the next century; and if deforestation substantially reduces tropical forests (as projected), a doubling of atmosphereic CO_2 could occur sooner. The result could be significant alterations of precipitation patterns around the world, and a 2°–3°C rise in temperatures in the middle latitudes of the earth. Agriculture and other human endeavors would have great difficulty in adapting to such large, rapid changes in climate. Even a 1°C increase in average global temperatures would make the earth's climate warmer than it has been any time in the last 1,000 years.

A carbon dioxide-induced temperature rise is expected to be 3 or 4 times greater at the poles than in the middle latitudes. An increase of 5°–10°C in polar temperatures could eventually lead to the melting of the Greenland and Antarctic ice caps and a gradual rise in sea level, forcing abandonment of many coastal cities.

Ozone is another major concern. The stratospheric ozone layer protects the earth from damaging ultraviolet light. However, the ozone layer is being threatened by chlorofluorocarbon emissions from aerosol cans and refrigeration equipment, by nitrous oxide (N_2O) emissions from the denitrification of both organic and inorganic nitrogen fertilizers, and possibly by the effects of high-altitude aircraft flights. Only the United States and a few other countries have made serious efforts to date to control the use of aerosol cans. Refrigerants and nitrogen fertilizers present even more difficult challenges. The most widely discussed effect of ozone depletion and the resulting increase in ultraviolet light is an increased incidence of skin cancer, but damage to food crops would also be significant and might actually prove to be the most serious ozone related problem.

Impacts of Nuclear Energy

The problems presented by the projected production of increasing amounts of nuclear power are different from but no less serious than those related to fossil fuel combustion. The risk of radioactive contamination of the environment due to nuclear power reactor accidents will be increased, as will the potential for proliferation of nuclear weapons. No nation has yet conducted a demonstration program for the satisfactory

disposal of radioactive wastes, and the amount of wastes is increasing rapidly. Several hundred thousand tons of highly radioactive spent nuclear fuel will be generated over the lifetimes of the nuclear plants likely to be constructed through the year 2000. In addition, nuclear power production will create millions of cubic meters of low-level radioactive wastes, and uranium mining and processing will lead to the production of hundreds of millions of tons of low-level radioactive tailings. It has not yet been demonstrated that all of these high- and low-level wastes from nuclear power production can be safely stored and disposed of without incident. Some of the by-products of reactors, it should be noted, have half-lives approximately five times as long as the period of recorded history.

Species Extinctions

Finally, the world faces an urgent problem of loss of plant and animal genetic resources. An estimate prepared for the Global 2000 Study suggests that between half a million and 2 million species—15 to 20 percent of all species on earth—could be extinguished by 2000, mainly because of loss of wild habitat but also in part because of pollution. Extinction of species on this scale is without precedent in human history.[63]

One-half to two-thirds of the extinctions projected to occur by 2000 will result from the clearing or degradation of tropical forests. Insect, other invertebrate, and plant species—many of them unclassified and unexamined by scientists—will account for most of the losses. The potential value of this genetic reservoir is immense. If preserved and carefully managed, tropical forest species could be a sustainable source of new foods (especially nuts and fruits), pharmaceutical chemicals, natural predators of pests, building materials, speciality woods, fuel, and so on. Even careful husbandry of the remaining biotic resources of the tropics cannot compensate for the swift, massive losses that are to be expected if present trends continue.

Current trends also threaten freshwater and marine species. Physical alterations—damming, channelization, siltation—and pollution by salts, acid rain, pesticides, and other toxic chemicals are profoundly affecting freshwater ecosystems throughout the world. At present 274 freshwater

38

vertebrate taxa are threatened with extinction, and by the year 2000 many may have been lost.

Some of the most important genetic losses will involve the extinction not of species but of subspecies and varieties of cereal grains. Four-fifths of the world's food supplies are derived from less than two dozen plant and animal species. Wild and local domestic strains are needed for breeding resistance to pests and pathogens into the high-yield varieties now widely used.

These varietal stocks are rapidly diminishing as marginal wild lands are brought into cultivation. Local domesticated varieties, often uniquely suited to local conditions, are also being lost as higher-yield varieties displace them. And the increasing practice of monoculture of a few strains—which makes crops more vulnerable to disease epidemics or plagues of pests—is occurring at the same time that the genetic resources to resist such disasters are being lost.

Entering the Twenty-First Century

The preceding sections have presented individually the many projections made by U.S. Government agencies for the Global 2000 Study. How are these projections to be interpreted collectively? What do they imply about the world's entry into the twenty-first century?[64]

The world in 2000 will be different from the world today in important ways. There will be more people. For every two persons on the earth in 1975 there will be three in 2000. The number of poor will have increased. Four-fifths of the world's population will live in less developed countries. Furthermore, in terms of persons per year added to the world, population growth will be 40 percent *higher* in 2000 than in 1975.[65]

The gap between the richest and the poorest will have increased. By every measure of material welfare the study provides—per capita GNP and consumption of food, energy, and minerals—the gap will widen. For example, the gap between the GNP per capita in the LDCs and the industrialized countries is projected to grow from about $4,000 in 1975 to about $7,900 in 2000.[66] Great disparities within countries are also expected to continue.

There will be fewer resources to go around. While on a worldwide average there was about four-tenths of a hectare of arable land per person in 1975, there will be only about one-quarter hectare per person in 2000[67] (see Figure 11 below). By 2000 nearly 1,000 billion barrels of the world's total original petroleum resource of approximately 2,000 billion barrels will have been consumed. Over just the 1975-2000 period, the world's remaining petroleum resources per capita can be expected to decline by at least 50 percent.[68] Over the same period world per capita water supplies will decline by 35 percent because of greater population alone; increasing competing demands will put further pressure on available water supplies.[69] The world's per capita growing stock of wood is projected to be 47 percent lower in 2000 than in 1978[70].

The environment will have lost important life-supporting capabilities. By 2000, 40 percent of the forests still remaining in the LDCs in 1978 will have been razed.[71] The atmospheric concentration of carbon dioxide will be nearly one-third higher than preindustrial levels.[72] Soil erosion will have removed, on the average, several inches of soil from croplands all over the world. Desertification (including salinization) may have claimed a significant fraction of the world's rangeland and cropland. Over little more than two decades, 15-20 percent of the earth's total species of plants and animals will have become extinct—a loss of at least 500,000 species.[73]

Prices will be higher. The price of many of the most vital resources is projected to rise in real terms—that is, over and above inflation. In order to meet projected demand, a 100 percent increase in the real price of food will be required.[74] To keep energy demand in line with anticipated supplies, the real price of energy is assumed to rise more than 150 percent over the 1975-2000 period.[75] Supplies of water, agricultural land, forest products, and many traditional marine fish species are projected to decline relative to growing demand at current prices,[76] which suggests that real price rises will occur in these sectors too. Collectively, the projections suggest that resource-based inflationary pressures will continue and intensify, especially in nations that are poor in resources or are rapidly depleting their resources.

The world will be more vulnerable both to natural disaster and to disruptions from human causes. Most nations are likely to be still more dependent on foreign sources of energy in 2000 than they are today.[77] Food production will be more vulnerable to disruptions of fossil fuel energy supplies and to weather fluctuations as cultivation expands to more marginal areas. The loss of diverse germ plasm in local strains and wild progenitors of food crops, together with the increase of monoculture, could lead to greater risks

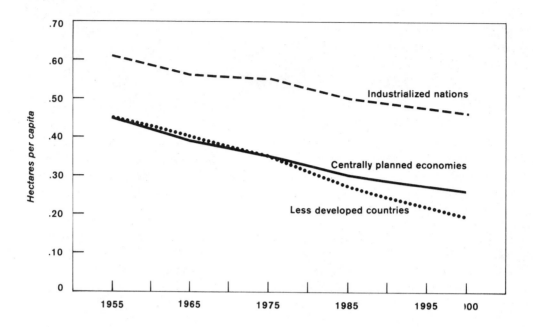

Figure 11. Arable land per capita, 1955, 1975, 2000.

of massive crop failures.[78] Larger numbers of people will be vulnerable to higher food prices or even famine when adverse weather occurs.[79] The world will be more vulnerable to the disruptive effects of war. The tensions that could lead to war will have multiplied. The potential for conflict over fresh water alone is underscored by the fact that out of 200 of the world's major river basins, 148 are shared by two countries and 52 are shared by three to ten countries. Long standing conflicts over shared rivers such as the Plata (Brazil, Argentina), Euphrates (Syria, Iraq), or Ganges (Bangladesh, India) could easily intensify.[80]

Finally, it must be emphasized that if public policy continues generally unchanged the world will be different as a result of lost opportunities. The adverse effects of many of the trends discussed in this Study will not be fully evident until 2000 or later; yet the actions that are necessary to change the trends cannot be postponed without foreclosing important options. The opportunity to stabilize the world's population below 10 billion, for example, is slipping away; Robert McNamara, President of the World Bank, has noted that for every decade of delay in reaching replacement fertility, the world's ultimately stabilized population will be about 11 percent greater.[81] Similar losses of opportunity accompany delayed perceptions or

action in other areas. If energy policies and decisions are based on yesterday's (or even today's) oil prices, the opportunity to wisely invest scarce capital resources will be lost as a consequence of undervaluing conservation and efficiency. If agricultural research continues to focus on increasing yields through practices that are highly energy-intensive, both energy resources and the time needed to develop alternative practices will be lost.

The full effects of rising concentrations of carbon dioxide, depletion of stratospheric ozone, deterioration of soils, increasing introduction of complex persistent toxic chemicals into the environment, and massive extinction of species may not occur until well after 2000. Yet once such global environmental problems are in motion they are very difficult to reverse. In fact, few if any of the problems addressed in the Global 2000 Study are amenable to quick technological or policy fixes; rather, they are inextricably mixed with the world's most perplexing social and economic problems.

Perhaps the most troubling problems are those in which population growth and poverty lead to serious long-term declines in the productivity of renewable natural resource systems. In some areas the capacity of renewable resource systems to support human populations is already being seriously damaged by efforts of present populations to meet desperate immediate needs, and the damage threatens to become worse.[82]

Examples of serious deterioration of the earth's most basic resources can already be found today in scattered places in all nations, including the industrialized countries and the better-endowed LDCs. For instance, erosion of agricultural soil and salinization of highly productive irrigated farmland is increasingly evident in the United States,[83] and extensive deforestation, with more or less permanent soil degradation, has occurred in Brazil, Venezuela, and Colombia.[84] But problems related to the decline of the earth's carrying capacity are most immediate, severe, and tragic in those regions of the earth containing the poorest LDCs.

Sub-Saharan Africa faces the problem of exhaustion of its resource base in an acute form. Many causes and effects have come together there to produce excessive demands on the environment, leading to expansion of the desert. Overgrazing, fuelwood gathering, and destructive cropping practices are the principal immediate causes of a series of transitions from open woodland, to scrub, to fragile semiarid range, to worthless weeds and bare earth. Matters are made worse when people are forced by scarcity of fuelwood to burn animal dung and crop wastes. The soil, deprived of organic matter, loses fertility and the ability to hold water—and the desert expands. In Bangladesh, Pakistan, and large parts of India, efforts by growing numbers of people to meet their basic needs are damaging the very cropland, pasture, forests, and water supplies on which they must depend for a livelihood.[85] To restore the lands and soils would require decades—if not centuries—*after* the existing pressures on the land have diminished. But the pressures are growing, not diminishing.

There are no quick or easy solutions, particularly in those regions where population pressure is already leading to a reduction of the carrying capacity of the land. In such regions a complex of social and economic factors (including very low incomes, inequitable land tenure, limited or no educational opportunities, a lack of non-agricultural jobs, and economic pressures toward higher fertility) underlies the decline in the land's carrying capacity. Furthermore, it is generally believed that social and economic conditions must improve before fertility levels will decline to replacement levels. Thus a vicious circle of causality may be at work. Environmental deterioration caused by large populations creates living conditions that make reductions in fertility difficult to achieve; all the while, continuing population growth increases further the pressures on the environment and land.[86]

The declines in carrying capacity already being observed in scattered areas around the world point to a phenomenon that could easily be much more widespread by 2000. In fact, the best evidence now available—even allowing for the many beneficial effects of technological developments and adoptions—suggests that by 2000 the world's human population may be within only a few generations of reaching the entire planet's carrying capacity.

The Global 2000 Study does not estimate the earth's carrying capacity, but it does provide a basis for evaluating an earlier estimate published in the U.S. National Academy of Sciences' report, *Resources and Man*. In this 1969 report, the Academy concluded that a world population of 10 billion "is close to (if not above) the maximum that an *intensively managed* world might hope to support with some degree of comfort and individual choice." The Academy also concluded that even with the sacrifice of individual freedom and choice, and even with chronic near starvation for the great majority, the human population of the world is unlikely to ever exceed 30 billion.[87]

Nothing in the Global 2000 Study counters the Academy's conclusions. If anything, data gathered over the past decade suggest the Academy may have underestimated the extent of some problems, especially deforestation and the loss and deterioration of soils.[88]

At present and projected growth rates, the world's population would rapidly approach the Academy's figures. If the fertility and mortality rates projected for 2000 were to continue unchanged into the twenty-first century, the world's population would reach 10 billion by 2030. Thus anyone with a present life expectancy of an additional 50 years could expect to see the world population reach 10 billion. This same rate of growth would produce a population of nearly 30 billion before the end of the twenty-first century.[89]

Here it must be emphasized that, unlike most

of the Global 2000 Study projections, the population projections assume extensive policy changes and developments to reduce fertility rates. Without the assumed policy changes, the projected rate of population growth would be still more rapid.

Unfortunately population growth may be slowed for reasons other than declining birth rates. As the world's populations exceed and reduce the land's carrying capacity in widening areas, the trends of the last century or two toward improved health and longer life may come to a halt. Hunger and disease may claim more lives— especially lives of babies and young children. More of those surviving infancy may be mentally and physically handicapped by childhood malnutrition.

The time for action to prevent this outcome is running out. Unless nations collectively and individually take bold and imaginative steps toward improved social and economic conditions, reduced fertility, better management of resources, and protection of the environment, the world must expect a troubled entry into the twenty-first century.

APPENDIX A

The Global 2000 Study Compared with Other Global Studies

In the course of the Global 2000 Study, the Government's several models (here referred to collectively as the "Government's global model") and their projections were compared with those of five other global studies.[90] The purpose was not only to compare the results of different projections, but also to see whether and how different assumptions and model structures may have led to different projections and findings.

The Global 2000 Study's principal findings are generally consistent with those of the five other global studies despite considerable differences in models and assumptions. On the whole, the other studies and their models lack the richness of detail that the Government's global model provides for the various individual sectors—food and agriculture, forests, water, energy, and so on. However, the linkages among the sectors in the other models are much more complete. Many apparent inconsistencies and contradictions in the Global 2000 projections are due to the weakness of the linkages among sectors of the Government's global model.

Another important difference is that the Government's projections stop at the year 2000 or before, while the other global studies project well into the twenty-first century. The most dramatic developments projected in the other studies—serious resource scarcities, population declines due to rising death rates, severe environmental deterioration—generally occur in the first half of the twenty-first century and thus cannot be compared with the Government's projections. Up to the turn of the century, all of the analyses, including the Government's, indicate more or less similar trends: continued economic growth in most areas, continued population growth everywhere, reduced energy growth, an increasingly tight and expensive food situation, increasing water problems, and growing environmental stress.

The most optimistic of the five models is the Latin American World Model. Instead of projecting future conditions on the basis of present policies and trends, this model asks: "How can global resources best be used to meet basic human needs for all people?" The model allocates labor and capital to maximize life expectancy. It assumes that personal consumption is sacrificed to maintain very high investment rates (25 percent of GNP per year), and it posits an egalitarian, nonexploitative, wisely managed world society that avoids pollution, soil depletion, and other forms of environmental degradation. Under these assumptions it finds that in little more than one generation basic human needs could be adequately satisfied in Latin America and in Africa. Thereafter, GNP would grow steadily and population growth would begin to stabilize.

But in Asia, even assuming these near-utopian social conditions and high rates of investment, the system collapses. The model projects an Asian food crisis beginning by 2010, as land runs out; food production cannot rise fast enough to keep up with population growth, and a vicious circle begins that leads to starvation and economic collapse by midcentury. The modelers suggest that an Asian food crisis could be avoided by such means as food imports from other areas with more cropland, better crop yields, and effective family planning policies. Nonetheless, it is striking that this model, which was designed to show that the fundamental constraints on human welfare were social, not physical, does project catastrophic food shortages in Asia due to land scarcity.

The World 2 and World 3 models, which were the basis of the 1972 Club of Rome report *The Limits to Growth*, give much attention to environmental factors—the only models in the group of five to do so. The World models, like the Global 2000 Study, considered trends in population, resources, and environment. However, these models are highly aggregated, looking at the world as a whole and omitting regional differences. In the cases that assume a continuation of present policies, the World 2 and 3 models project large global increases in food and income per capita until 2020, at which time either food scarcity or resource depletion would cause a downturn. The two models do suggest that major changes of policy can significantly alter these trends.

The World Integrated Model, a later effort sponsored by the Club of Rome, is much more detailed than the World 2 and 3 models in its treatment of regional differences, trade, economics, and shifts from one energy source to another, but it is less inclusive in its treatment of the environment. This complex model has been run under many different assumptions of conditions and policies. Almost invariably the runs project a long-term trend of steeply rising food prices. Under a wide range of policies and conditions the runs indicate massive famine in Asia and, to a lesser degree, in non-OPEC Africa, before the turn of the century.

The United Nations World Model found that to meet U.N. target rates for economic growth, developing countries would have to make great sacrifices in personal consumption, saving and investing at unprecedented rates. Personal consumption would not exceed 63 percent of income in any developing region, and none would have a level of private investment of less than 20 percent. To meet food requirements, global agricultural production would have to rise fourfold by 2000, with greater increases required in many places (500 percent, for example, in low-income Asia and Latin America).

The Model of International Relations in Agriculture (MOIRA) confines itself to agriculture; it takes into account the effects of agriculture policies but not those of environmental degradation. Its results are more optimistic than the Global 2000 projections: world food production more than doubles from 1975 to 2000, and per capita consumption rises 36 percent. Even so, because of unequal distribution, the number of people subsisting on two-thirds or less of the biological protein requirement rises from 350 million in 1975 to 740 million in 2000.

The Global 2000 Study conducted an experiment with two of the more integrated nongovernment models to answer the question: "How would projections from the Government's global model be different if the model were more integrated and included more linkages and feedback?" The linkages in the two nongovernment models were severed so that they bore some resemblance to the unconnected and inconsistent structure of the Government's global model. Chosen for the experiment were the World 3 model and the World Integrated Model.

In both models, severing the linkages led to distinctly more favorable outcomes. On the basis of results with World 3, the Global 2000 Study concluded that a more integrated Government model would project that:

- Increasing competition among agriculture, industry, and energy development for capital would lead to even higher resource cost inflation and significant decreases in real GNP growth (this assumes no major technological advances).

- The rising food prices and regional declines in food consumption per capita that are presently projected would be intensified by competition for capital and by degradation of the land.

- Slower GNP and agricultural growth would lead to higher death rates from widespread hunger—or from outright starvation—and to higher birth rates, with greater numbers of people trapped in absolute poverty.

- A decisive global downturn in incomes and food per capita would probably not take place until a decade or two after 2000 (this assumes no political disruptions).

When links in the World Integrated Model (WIM) were cut, outcomes again were more favorable. The results of the unlinked version were comparable to the Global 2000 quantitative projections for global GNP, population, grain production, fertilizer use, and energy use. But in the original integrated version of WIM, gross world product was 21 percent lower than in the unlinked version—$11.7 trillion instead of $14.8 trillion in 2000. In the linked version, world agricultural production rose 85 percent instead of 107 percent; grain available for human consumption rose less than 85 percent because some of the grain was fed to animals for increased meat production. Population rose only to 5.9 billion rather than 6.2 billion, in part because of widespread starvation (158 million deaths cumulatively by 2000) and in part because of lower birth rates in the industrialized countries. The effects of severing the linkages are much less in lightly populated regions with a wealth of natural resources, such as North America, than in regions under stress, where great numbers of people are living at the margin of existence. In North America, the difference in GNP per capita was about 5 percent; in South Asia, about 30 percent.

The inescapable conclusion is that the omission of linkages imparts an optimistic bias to the Global 2000 Study's (and the U.S. Government's) quantitative projections.[91] This appears to be particularly true of the GNP projections. The experiments with the World Integrated Model suggest that the Study's figure for gross world product in 2000 may be 15—20 percent too high.

APPENDIX B

Letter of Transmittal

The President

Sir: In your Environmental Message to the Congress of May 23, 1977, you directed the Council on Environmental Quality and the Department of State, working with other federal agencies, to study the "probable changes in the world's population, natural resources, and environment through the end of the century." This endeavor was to serve as "the foundation of our longer-term planning."

The effort we then undertook to project present world trends and to establish a foundation for planning is now complete, and we are pleased to present our report to you. What emerges are not predictions but rather projections developed by U.S. Government agencies of what will happen to population, resources, and environment if present policies continue.

Our conclusions, summarized in the pages that follow, are disturbing. They indicate the potential for global problems of alarming proportions by the year 2000. Environmental, resource, and population stresses are intensifying and will increasingly determine the quality of human life on our planet. These stresses are already severe enough to deny many millions of people basic needs for food, shelter, health, and jobs, or any hope for betterment. At the same time, the earth's carrying capacity—the ability of biological systems to provide resources for human needs—is eroding. The trends reflected in the Global 2000 Study suggest strongly a progressive degradation and improverishment of the earth's natural resource base.

If these trends are to be altered and the problems diminished, vigorous, determined new initiatives will be required worldwide to meet human needs while protecting and restoring the earth's capacity to support life. Basic natural resources—farmlands, fisheries, forests, minerals, energy, air, and water—must be conserved and better managed. Changes in public policy are needed around the world before problems worsen and options for effective action are reduced.

A number of responses to global resource, environment, and population problems—responses only touched on in the Study—are underway. Heightened international concern is reflected in the "Megaconferences" convened by the United Nations during the last decade: Human Environment (1972), Population (1974), Food (1974), Human Settlements (1976), Water (1977), Desertification (1977), Science and Technology for Development (1979), and New and Renewable Sources of Energy, scheduled for August 1981 in Nairobi. The United States has contributed actively to these conferences, proposing and supporting remedial actions of which many are now being taken. We are also working with other nations bilaterally, building concern for population growth, natural resources, and environment into our foreign aid programs and cooperating with our immediate neighbors on common problems ranging from cleanup of air and water pollution to preservation of soils and development of new crops. Many nations around the world are adopting new approaches—replanting deforested areas, conserving energy, making family planning measures widely available, using natural predators and selective pesticides to protect crops instead of broadscale destructive application of chemicals.

Nonetheless, given the urgency, scope, and complexity of the challenges before us, the efforts now underway around the world fall far short of what is needed. An era of unprecedented global cooperation and commitment is essential.

The necessary changes go beyond the capability of any single nation. But our nation can itself take important and exemplary steps. Because of our preeminent position as a producer and consumer of food and energy, our efforts to conserve soil, farmlands, and energy resources are of global, as well as national, importance. We can avoid polluting our own environment, and we must take care that we do not degrade the global environment.

Beyond our borders we can expand our collaboration with both developed and developing nations in a spirit of generosity and justice. Hundreds of millions of the world's people are now trapped in a condition of abject poverty. People at the margin of existence must take cropland, grazing land, and fuel where they can find it, regardless of the effects upon the earth's resource base. Sustainable economic development, coupled with environmental protection, resource management, and family planning is essential. Equally important are better understanding and effective responses to such global problems as the buildup of carbon dioxide in the atmosphere and the threat of species loss on a massive scale.

Finally, to meet the challenges described in the Global 2000 Study our federal government requires a much stronger capability to project and analyze long-term trends. The Study clearly points to the need for improving the present foundation for long-term planning. On this foundation rest decisions that involve the future welfare of the Nation.

We wish to express our thanks to and our admiration for the Director of the Global 2000 Study, Dr. Gerald O. Barney and his staff. Their diligence, dedication, and ability to bring forth the best from a legion of contributors is much appreciated. Special thanks is also due to those of the Council on Environmental Quality and the Department of State who worked closely with the Study and to the 11 other agencies that contributed greatly to it.* Without the detailed knowledge provided by these agencies' experts, the Global 2000 Study would have been impossible.

Respectfully,

THOMAS R. PICKERING
Assistant Secretary, Oceans and
   International Environmental
   and Scientific Affairs,
Department of State

GUS SPETH
Chairman,
Council on Environmental
Quality

---

*The Federal agencies that cooperated with us in this effort were the Departments of Agriculture, Energy, and the Interior, the Agency for International Development, the Central Intelligence Agency, the Environmental Protection Agency, the Federal Emergency Management Agency, the National Aeronautics and Space Administration, the National Science Foundation, the National Oceanic and Atmospheric Administration, and the Office of Science and Technology Policy.

APPENDIX C

The Institute for 21st Century Studies

The Institute for 21st Century Studies—an independent, nonprofit, charitable, and educational organization—was launched in 1985 with initial funding from the Rockefeller Brothers Fund. The Institute's primary mission is to assist both industrialized and developing nations in the exploration of strategies for sustainable development and security.

To accomplish this mission the Institute provides support for the global network of national twenty-first century study teams described in the Preface to the Revised Edition. Specifically, the Institute

- Identifies individuals who want to start twenty-first-century studies for their countries and assists them in launching these studies.
- Trains teams in the general methodology of doing studies on alternative futures.
- Participates, when needed, in the design and analysis stages of a specific study.
- Raises questions during a study to direct attention to issues of sustainability.
- Provides the teams with information about specific strategies for sustainable development and security.
- Acts as liaison between the teams and organizations that can assist with specific aspects of the studies and their implementation.
- Gathers, analyzes, and passes on tools, such as microcomputer models, that will be useful to the teams in their work.

- Assists the teams in the publication and international distribution of their reports.
- Helps the teams identify steps that must be taken to ensure that their reports receive high-level attention and are used in national policy development.
- Organizes meetings at which the heads of the twenty-first-century studies meet and exchange information.

The Institute maintains a library of twenty-first-century study reports and a library of microcomputer software useful both in preparing twenty-first-century studies and in the general task of managing a nation. It has also published a book, *Managing a Nation: The Software Sourcebook*, which reviews the best software in its library. A second, greatly expanded version of this book will be published in late 1988 by Butterworth Scientific, Ltd.

For further information on the Institute, please write to or call the North American or European offices:

Institute for 21st Century Studies
1611 North Kent Street
Suite 610
Arlington, Virginia 22209-2111, USA
(703) 841-0048

REFERENCES

1. *The Global 2000 Report to the President: Entering the Twenty-First Century,* vol. 2, *Technical Report,* Gerald O. Barney, Study Director, Washington: Government Printing Office, 1980, App. A.
2. Ibid.
3. Jimmy Carter, *The President's Environmental Program, 1977,* Washington: Government Printing Office, May 1977, p. M-11.
4. A more detailed discussion of the Global 2000 Study process is provided in *The Global 2000 Report to the President,* vol. 2, *Technical Report,* "Preface and Acknowledgments" and Ch. 1, "Introduction to the Projections."
5. *The Global 2000 Report to the President: Entering the Twenty-First Century,* vol. 2, Ch. 14–23; and *The Global 2000 Report to the President: Entering the Twenty-First Century,* vol. 3, *The Government's Global Model,* Gerald O. Barney, Study Director, Washington: Government Printing Office, 1980.

NOTE

Unless otherwise indicated, the following chapter citations refer to the various chapters of *The Global 2000 Report to the President: Entering the Twenty-First Century,* vol. 2, *Technical Report,* Washington: Government Printing Office, 1980.

6. Ch. 13, 14, and 31.
7. Ch. 1.
8. "Closing the Loops," Ch. 13; Ch. 14.
9. Ibid.
10. Ch. 13, especially "Closing the Loops."
11. "Closing the Loops," Ch. 13; Ch. 14 and 31.
12. Ch. 1, 5, 14, and 23.
13. Ch. 1 and 14.
14. Ch. 30 and 31.
15. Ch. 2.
16. Ibid.
17. Ibid.
18. Ibid.
19. Ibid.; "Population Projections and the Environment," Ch. 13.
20. "Population Projections and the Environment." Ch. 13.
21. Ibid.; "Closing the Loops," Ch. 13.
22. Ibid.
23. *The Global 2000 Report to the President,* vol. 3, *The Government's Global Model,* Chapter on population models and the population projections update.
24. Ronald Freedman, "Theories of Fertility Decline: A Reappraisal," in Philip M. Hauser, ed., *World Population and Development,* Syracuse, N.Y.: Syracuse University Press, 1979; John C. Caldwell, "Toward a Restatement of Demographic Transition Theory," *Population and Development Review,* Sept./Dec., 1976.
25. For a discussion of Indonesia, see Freeman, op. cit.; for a discussion of Brazil, see "Demographic Projections Show Lower Birth Rate for the Poor" (in Portuguese), *VEJA,* Oct. 24, 1979, p. 139, citing the research of Elza Berquo of the Brazilian Analysis and Planning Center.
26. Ch. 3.
27. Ibid.
28. Ibid.
29. World Bank, *Prospects for Developing Countries, 1977–85,* Washington, Sept. 1976, Statistical Appendix, Table 1; World Bank, *World Development Report, 1979,* Washington, 1979, p. 13.
30. Ch. 6.
31. Ibid., "Food and Agriculture Projections and the Environment," Ch. 13.
32. Ch. 6.
33. Ibid.
34. "Food and Agriculture Projections and the Environment," Ch. 13.
35. Ch. 6.
36. U.S. Department of Agriculture, *Farm Income Statistics,* Washington: Economics, Statistics, and Cooperative Services, U.S.D.A., 1978 and 1979.
37. J. B. Penn, "The Food and Agriculture Policy Challenge of the 1980's," Washington: Economics, Statistics and Cooperative Service, U.S.D.A., Jan. 1980.
38. P. Osam, *Accelerating Foodgrain Production in Low-Income Food-Deficit Countries—Progress, Potentials and Paradoxes,* Hawaii: East-West Center, May 1978; J. Gravan, *The Calorie Energy Gap in Bangladesh, and Strategies for Reducing It,* Washington: International Food Policy Research Institute, Aug. 1977.
39. Ch. 7.
40. Ibid.; "The Projections and the Marine Environment" and "Water Projections and the Environment," Ch. 13.
41. Ch. 7.
42. Food and Agriculture Organization, *Fisheries Statistics Yearbook, 1978.* Rome, 1979; Richard Hennemuth, Deputy Director, Northeast Fisheries Center, National Oceanic and Atmospheric Administration, personal communication, 1980.
43. Ch. 8 and App. C.
44. Ibid.
45. Ibid.; "Population Projections and the Environment," "Forestry Projections and the Environment," and "Energy Projections and the Environment," Ch. 13.
46. Norman Myers, *The Sinking Ark,* New York: Pergamon Press, 1979; U.S. Department of State, *Proceedings of the U.S. Strategy Conference on Tropical Deforestation,* Washington, Oct. 1978.
47. See especially Ch. 2, 6, 9, 10, and 12.
48. Ch. 9.
49. Ibid.; "Water Projections and the Environment," Ch. 13.
50. Ch. 9 and 13.
51. Ch. 12.
52. Ibid.
53. Ibid.
54. Ibid.; "Nonfuel Minerals Projections and the Environment," Ch. 13.
55. Ch. 10; "Energy Projections and the Environment," Ch. 13.
56. Ibid.
57. Ibid.
58. Ch. 8; "Population Projections and the Environment," "Forestry Projections and the Environment," and "Energy Projections and the Environment," Ch. 13.
59. Ch. 8; "Forestry Projections and the Environment," "Energy Projections and the Environment," and "Clos-

ing the Loops,'' Ch. 13.

60. See the IEES Model Projections reported in "International Energy Assessment," in Energy Information Administration, *Annual Report to Congress, 1978,* vol. 3, Washington: Department of Energy, 1979, pp. 11–34; Energy Information Administration, *Annual Report to the Congress, 1979,* forthcoming.

61. See Energy Information Administration, *Annual Report, 1979,* op. cit.; John Pearson and Derriel Cato, personal communication, Mar. 13, 1980.

62. The discussion of "Environmental Consequences" that follows is based on Ch. 13.

63. Thomas E. Lovejoy, "A Projection of Species Extinctions," Ch. 13, pp. 328-31.

64. This section is based largely on material contained in "Closing the Loops," Ch. 13.

65. Ch. 2.

66. Ch. 3.

67. Ch. 6.

68. Ch. 10; "Energy Projections and the Environment," Ch. 13.

69. Ch. 9.

70. Ch. 8.

71. Ibid.; "Forestry Projections and the Environment," Ch. 13.

72. Ch. 4; "Climate Projections and the Environment," Ch. 13.

73. "Food and Agriculture Projections and the Environment," "Forestry Projections and the Environment," and "Closing the Loops," Ch. 13.

74. Ch. 6.

75. Extrapolating from Ch. 10, which assumes a 5 percent per year increase over the 1980–90 period.

76. Ch. 6–9.

77. Ch. 10 and 11.

78. Ch. 6; "Food and Agriculture Projections and the Environment," Ch. 13.

79. Ibid.; Ch. 4; "Climate Projections and the Environment," Ch. 13.

80. Ch. 9.

81. Robert S. McNamara, President, World Bank, "Address to the Board of Governors," Belgrade, Oct. 2, 1979, pp. 9, 10.

82. Ch. 13.

83. "Food and Agriculture Projections and the Environment," Ch. 13.

84. "Forestry Projections and the Environment," Ch. 13, and Peter Freeman, personal communication, 1980, based on field observations in 1973.

85. "Population Projections and the Environment," "Food and Agriculture Projections and the Environment," "Forestry Projections and the Environment," and "Water Projections and the Environment," Ch. 13.

86. "Population Projections and the Environment," and "Closing the Loops," Ch. 13; Erik Eckholm, *The Dispossessed of the Earth: Land Reform and Sustainable Development,* Washington: Worldwatch Institute, June 1979.

87. National Academy of Sciences, Committee on Resources and Man, *Resources and Man,* San Francisco: Freeman, 1969, p. 5; "Closing the Loops," Ch. 13.

88. "Closing the Loops," Ch. 13.

89. Projection by the U.S. Bureau of the Census communicated in a personal letter, Feb. 26, 1980, from Dr. Samuel Baum, Chief, International Demographic Data Center. This letter and projection are presented in vol. 3 of the *Global 2000 Report to the President,* Population section.

90. The discussion in this Appendix is based on the detailed analyses in Ch. 24–31 and on two papers by Jennifer Robinson (author of those chapters) presented at the International Conference on Modeling Related to Environment, sponsored by the Polish Academy of Sciences: "The Global 2000 Study: An Attempt to Increase Consistency in Government Forecasting" and "Treatment of the Environment in Global Models."

91. Further discussion of these and other potential biases in the Government's projections are provided in Ch. 14–23, and App. B.